PEOPLE ARE TALKING

"In today's world whe̶... ...nd pasted in an instant, it's cr... ...w to be safe, smart and ethical digita... ...ook provides parents with practical tips and ... ...each their kids how to thrive in the digital world."
    -**Caroline Knorr, Parenting Editor, Common Sense Media**

"In addition to using Instagram, Twitter and Facebook as a portfolio, Josh gives students pointers that helped to keep their information private. Everyone gets a clear road map that they can use to make sure they shine online."
    -**Tracy Rampy, Educational Technology, Southeast Kansas Education Service Center, Greenbush**

"Our kids were relieved to have someone tell them, "Hey, it's great to use it (social media) and you can brand yourself in a positive way for future college, career and volunteer endeavors." Rather than "It's bad, stay away from it, etc..." Josh enlightened many students and adults to things we had never considered on the topic of safety. This is one great proactive way we can combat cyber bullying; showing kids how to do it right and explaining how doing it "the other way" can have a lasting impact beyond getting in trouble with your parents or school."
    -**Mollie McNally, Assistant Principal, Blue Valley High School**

PEOPLE ARE TALKING

"Josh Ochs talks about students being more conscious of what they post and using social media to impress colleges and employers. As Ochs put it, 'every post is like a button on an
elevator, having the ability to take someone up or down. Anything that takes someone down is a wasted post, he says."
-Colleen Williamson, Senior Reporter, Parsons Sun Publishing

"Excellent advice for anyone that wants to improve their digital image and footprint. Essential for those on a job search."
-Lisa Cochrane, Senior Vice President of Marketing, Allstate Insurance Corp.

"Josh has created a formula students can use to build an online portfolio that helps them stand out in positive way."
-Julie Mossler, Head of Global Communications, Waze (acquired by Google)

"Josh's advice is practical. This is a MUST read for those applying for college."
-James Ellis, Dean of the USC Marshall School of Business

"This book will help you think differently about your digital footprint."
-Satnam Narang, Senior Security Response Manager, Symantec

As Josh's former boss and Brand Manager at the Walt Disney Company, I have witnessed Josh's people skills and seen him grow for over a decade. I sent Josh difficult projects because his ability to win the goodwill of our executives was an advantage to our company. In my experience, he has the credibility to be leading your kids to shine online. I'm pleased to see Josh sharing his winning strategies so freely.
–John Hanna
Former Brand Manager
The Walt Disney Company

BY THE SAME AUTHOR

Light, Bright and Polite:
How Businesses And Professionals Can Safely And
Effectively Navigate Social Media

Light, Bright and Polite®

How to Use Social Media

to Impress Colleges and

Future Employers

by Josh Ochs

MediaLeaders.com Publishing

This book is dedicated to my Grandma, Nadine.
I'll always cherish talking with you before my speeches.
I love you.

CONTENTS

DEAR READER

Thank you for reading this book. I am honored that you would take the time to listen to my message. I hope that you will register this book for free at SafeSmartSocial.com/book. We will send you videos and tools to help your students use social media to impress colleges and employers.

As an added bonus, we will email you all of the key takeaways from the book that you can use as a cheat-sheet in the future.

Thank you for taking the time to register your book and support my work,

@JoshOchs

INTRODUCTION

Over the past several years, I have had the great opportunity to work with some of the world's best brands. My staff and I developed and implemented techniques to help these companies shine online. And they have! By employing a few social media strategies, these great companies are finding the customers they want and deserve.

It quickly came to my attention that my techniques would be valuable to families who are preparing their kids for college. Many kids have no idea how their digital footprint might be viewed by others and how others' perceptions can hold them back.

During a 2013 Kaplan telephone questionnaire, 31% of college admissions officers said that they did visit applicants Facebook and other social media pages to gain more information on the student. 30% said that they had encountered information on social media that had a negative influence on an applicant's chance of being accepted. This goes to show that anything we put online, no matter how long ago, can be brought up on the first page of Google results and we need to be vigilant on what we allow others to see.[1]

In this book, you will receive the same strategies I've used to help many successful companies, but tailored to students and future leaders, to help them impress colleges and future

---

1. "Kaplan Test Prep," *Kaplan.com*, last modified October 31, 2013, SafeSmartSocial.com/research.

employers. As I've traveled the country for the past year and spoken to over 20,000 students, the feedback has been clear: these methods work, helping kids convey their best selves online. These methods employed keep their online images and communications *Light, Bright and Polite®*, which allows colleges and employers find the best people to represent their campus upon graduation. Your kid can be among them.

It's a competitive market out there, so let's not be disqualified from something to which you're aspiring without ever having a real chance at interviewing for the opportunity!

It is never too early to start planning ahead. Your kids may not be thinking about it, but certainly you understand from experience that what you do now can have lasting effects. At the very least, what you do now lays the foundation for the habits that you will have years from now.

Even if your children are not on social media yet, their reputation online starts as soon as their friends are online and posting photos of them, tagging them.

So, there's a lot to consider! Since parents have limited time, this book isn't designed to teach everything about social media. I'm not here to give you a list of 100 things not to do on social media. Instead, my goal is to have students and parents skim through this book and be able to pick up one or two helpful tips that can make all the difference.

What accomplishments does your kid want to have in the next five years?

- Getting into college
- Full ride scholarship
- Varsity sports team
- Study abroad opportunity
- Leadership award
- Community service
- Getting into a prestigious private high school
- Getting an internship that launches their career

If any of these apply, then you need to pay attention to all of the messages that your child sends out on social media. There's a good chance that 50% of their tweets might not be helping them to reach their goals. They need to be vigilant.

How do you get the most from this book?

I have also created dozens of videos that you can unlock for free when you register your book.

Visit SafeSmartSocial.com/book to register your copy for free and I will send you videos and tools to help your students use social media to impress colleges and employers. As an added bonus, when you register, I will email you all of the key takeaways from the book that you can use as a cheat-sheet in the future. Also, while this book uses footnotes and a bibliography, I understand that it would be cumbersome to type out web links if you want to visit the source material yourself. With that in mind, I've created a page at SafeSmartSocial.com/research where these links will be located and updated for easy click-throughs.

Lastly, to get your social media accounts started with positive images I encourage you to take a *Light, Bright and Polite*® photo of you holding this book. Then tag me (@ JoshOchs) in the Instagram or Twitter message and I'll share the image on my Twitter account to 50,000+ followers.

Thank you for supporting my book and for taking the next step to shine online,

Josh Ochs
@JoshOchs

PREFACE

Parents: If your kids are lashing out on social media, please consider having a dialogue with them. The ideas in this book are not right for kids who are being bullied or are using social media as a way to express their feelings.

Kids: If you are being bullied or want to talk about something with a live person, here's a couple numbers you can call. There are real people that will listen to your concerns instead of you sharing it on social media.

Consider phoning a crisis help line about anything you need to share or for which you need help, that you would never want to go public. Keep in mind, and make sure that your kids are aware of, toll-free support lines to call during times of stress and feelings of hopelessness:

1-800-273-TALK (8255) Suicide Prevention Lifeline

(205) 328-5437 Kids Help Line, a division of Crisis Center in Birmingham, AL. They state that anyone can phone 2-3 times a day to talk about any needs. To avoid long distance charges, one can phone from a Gmail account for free, or other VOIP services.

CrisisChat.org - This is an online chat service to talk with someone from your computer.

CHAPTER ONE
How social media can hurt your kid's future

Everywhere I go, I'm second to arrive. My reputation precedes me, and sometimes it skips out on the bill. – Jarod Kintz

---

Almost every student has heard a horror story. At the start of the school year, a BASIS college counselor told her class of a student whose acceptance to an elite college was revoked when he was caught badmouthing the school on Facebook. At Williams College, a student's admission was rescinded because he posted disparaging remarks on a college discussion board. At the University of Georgia, when an admissions officer discovered an applicant's racially charged Twitter account, he took a screenshot and added the tweets to the student's application file.[1]

If you think that your kids don't have many followers and they will never get found, consider learning more about Justine Sacco's careless tweet while boarding a 14-hour plane ride. She went from having less than 200 followers to being the number one trending hashtag on Twitter before her

---

1. Victor Luckerson, "When Colleges Look Up Applicants on Facebook: The Unspoken New Admissions Test," *Time.com*, last modified November 15, 2012, SafeSmartSocial.com/research.

plane ever landed—which means that millions of people saw it. Whether you believe she was careless or being unfairly picked upon, one thing can't be denied: social media allows thousands of people to create a flash mob of comments that can ruin an online image in a very short amount of time.[2]

Have you ever applied for a job, scholarship or opportunity you really wanted, thinking you were a shoo-in, but then never heard back and wondered why? Why, when you're so great, and when your presentation was so good, and you were so qualified, did you not get a call back? Maybe your karma was on hiatus, maybe someone even more qualified knocked it out of the park, or maybe it was a case of SOK: The Silent Opportunity Killer.

Although social media can be used for good, and should be used, it isn't very forgiving. Posts you've forgotten and assumed were hidden, because new content replaced it, can be easily found. Even deleted posts can be found (we'll cover this at the end of the chapter) and can completely change someone's idea of your kid. Ill-timed, tone-deaf, poorly-worded, impulsive, unkind, or just inaccurately representative posts can harm one's reputation and if found by potential employers or colleges, they can silently smother your opportunity to death.

With so many social media sites—Tumblr, Snapchat, Yik Yak, Facebook, Twitter, Instagram, Pinterest, Vine, Medium— tweens and teens create and send a lot of social media posts. This means a lot of opportunity for them to mess up. Are they always on guard? Are they always keeping it Light, Bright and Polite®? If they are using Snapchat, probably not, since they are lulled into a sense of safety by its built-in content expiration feature. However, people can, in one second, take

---

2. Jon Ronson, "How One Stupid Tweet Blew Up Justine Sacco's Life," *New York Times*, last modified February 12, 2015, SafeSmartSocial.com/research.

a screenshot of a Snapchat photo before it expires, and post it somewhere to exist forever.

You're only as good as your last 10 tweets and/or your first page of your Google results. Those first posts or tweets popping up on your kid's profile are what will leave the most lasting impression. Each tweet, with the right circumstances, has the possibility of getting them fired or removed from the college application process, or booted out even after formal acceptance. It's important, too, for your kid to keep being Light, Bright and Polite® well after their first semester. They've still got internships, study abroad, and jobs to compete for.

Making my case

You might be thinking, "I'm not too worried. My kid doesn't post nude photos or party photos or curse people out or say blatantly racist things online." But what you need to know is that it's not enough to also avoid posts that are well-known to be controversial. Even if they avoid ambiguous jokes that could be construed as racist or abusive, other dangers are especially hard to avoid for young people growing up with social media. Their identities are unstable, still being formed. Information they don't mind people knowing about them at age 14 can change a lot by age 18. Their opinions change. Their goals change as they are exposed to new experiences. As their brains develop into their 20s, they close in on having better control over their impulses.

> Reports show that over 30% of colleges are going to search for your kids online.

They may simply be posting content that distracts from their goal by failing to align with the overall impression they want to leave upon admissions advisors.

"This student has a slightly lower GPA than her peers, but I looked at her Instagram profile and she has

25 selfies and a lot of comments from her friends....I bet she's really fun and a great person. Out of the hundreds of other candidates, let's give her one of the few second round interviews and trust that she's a better candidate than someone with a more professional online image,"

said no one in admissions, ever.

Your kid could have the highest grades in their class, but if someone finds their photos from pie-eating contests, backyard barbecues and harmless tailgating at sporting events, these won't contribute to the image they are trying to create of someone who is studious, accomplished, charitable and who takes good care of themselves. There's nothing wrong with looking like someone who knows how to have a good time, but schools are looking for students, not fun-time folks. It's important for the content to approximately reflect the image you want employers and advisors to have. 90% studious, 10% fun-haver, not the other way around.

Let's say that your kid does a good job with their social media-framed identity and they get accepted into college. Their job isn't over yet! They must remain vigilant at monitoring their image because they can still be rejected.

The New York Times interviewed Colgate's dean of admissions Gary L. Ross on the college acceptance process. Apparently, Colgate had offered a student acceptance, until they saw him connected to an alcohol related incident online. The student was contacted, and verified that the details of the incident, and his admission was rescinded. This goes to show that online is a public domain to which everyone has access.[3]

---

3. Natasha Singer, "They Loved Your GPA Then They Saw Your Tweets," *New York Times*, last modified November 9, 2013, SafeSmartSocial.com/research.

Remember: There are other kids who are trying to get into the same prestigious, elite colleges that your child is targeting. They have also worked hard in high school, taken advanced classes and participated in community service and extracurricular activities. They may even have a 4.0 GPA, or higher (just like your child). The other student's big advantage may be that they were aware of their online image, and they were proactive to maintain a clean online presence.

Here's an analogy: Your kids are paving a yellow brick road that's easy to follow. In the 1939 movie *The Wizard of Oz*, Dorothy is told that if she stays on the yellow brick road, she'll find out more about the wizard that she's looking for. Your kid's social media presence is much like that yellow brick road. Colleges are like Dorothy and your kid is the wizard. Each one of your kids' posts is like one of the bricks. Together they form a windy road that colleges can follow to discover more about who your kid really is. Imagine if some of the bricks were grey jagged rock instead of blocks of gold. The design flaw of the grey rocks would be so noticeable, that they would stand out in memory, and perhaps Dorothy would leave the road for another yellow brick road nearby, with flawless paving. We want to keep Dorothy, er, those colleges, on that path, brick-by-yellow-brick until they settle upon an idea of who the Wizard—the athlete, the volunteer, the artist, the deserving applicant—really is: your kid.

> *Without leaps of imagination, or dreaming, we lose the excitement of possibilities. Dreaming, after all, is a form of planning.*
> - Gloria Steinam

Planning ahead

If your kids are young, it might be a good time to start working on a ten year plan with them. It doesn't have to be anything concrete right now while they're 6 or 7, but the foundation should be laid and it should come into sharper focus as they get older. What clubs do they want to participate in during middle school? What sports do they want to play? For some school systems, students are introduced to competitive sports by the 8th grade, if not sooner. If you and your child are serious about getting into a sport, it should start now.

If they want to go to a private high school, they need to be building a portfolio of accomplishments in middle school by involving themselves win clubs, teams, the wider community, religious organizations, etc. All of that can start even before they get to middle school.

In the coming years, resumes are going to be a thing of the past. Your kid's new online image is going to be owned by Google and any other large search engine that wants to keep a copy of your kid's data. The first place colleges and employers are going to visit when researching your kids will be Google, YouTube, Google Images, Facebook, Instagram, Twitter and any other new networks making their information public.

How posted content can haunt forever

Have you ever used a whiteboard only to realize that you accidentally grabbed a permanent marker instead of a dry erase marker? It would have been so simple and easy to double-check but it's also easy to not think to check. Posting online can be like that. A permanent message on a whiteboard is embarrassing to leave in the office for everyone to see, but it can be cleaned up (Pro tip: by writing over top with a dry erase marker!). Social media can be forever.

Maybe you're thinking, *But the internet is so big! How do they find so much on you? What if you delete stuff?* If only it were so simple.

First, it's important to understand how search works on Google. Sure, if someone just searches your name, particularly if you have a common last name like "Smith," there may not be much to be found. But let's say your kid is David Smith, living in New York City. He goes to Super Duper High School where he plays basketball. He likes Morrissey. The admissions advisor could search a combo of that information and find a Tumblr account, a blog, or a profile on a Morrissey fan message board. On the message board, he uses a "handle": SuperDuper567. The admissions advisor now tries searching "SuperDuper567," knowing that people tend to reuse the same handle in other places online. The advisor finds David's YouTube account. He's left some mean comments on some videos. Oops!

David can also be found by searching his email address. A friend of mine was excited to be going on a date with an up-and-coming young poet who had recently won a major national poetry award. She Googled him by searching his email address and found a LiveJournal blog he started at age 19. He was now in his 30s and was very embarrassed to have it still visible publicly and so easily findable.

> *The question isn't 'What do we want to know about people?' It's, 'What do people want to tell about themselves?*
> – Mark Zuckerberg, Facebook Founder

That's not all! You also need to know about ways that content is made permanent, etched in internet stone:

1. **The Wayback Machine.** archive.org/web/ keeps a copy of every website by taking a snapshot of it. If your kid has or had a blog, type the blog address into the search bar on this page. Next, it will say how many captures there are. Click on that link, and you'll see calendars of each month, with some dates in blue circles. You can click on those dates and see a snapshot of the blog. You can navigate throughout the blog as if you were on the site itself. The only way to get rid of this archive is to own the domain (website address) for the page forever and prove it to the Internet Archive staff and ask them to disclude the address from their archive.

2. **Google's cache.** Google also takes a snapshot of every web page and keeps it available in a cache. When

you search for anything on Google, you'll often see a little down-pointing arrow besides the green link underneath the web page title. If you click on the arrow, you'll see the "cached" option. This means that even if your kid deletes information on social media site, it might still come up in the search results, in the cache, available to view as a snapshot of the page. Sometimes you can get Google to delete pages from their cache if it's causing damage, but it's not easy.

3. **Screenshots.** The Internet is like the Wild West. Post something on social media that someone thinks is controversial or incriminating and within seconds someone may have taken a screenshot—which is like a photo—of the post and automatically saved it to their computer's desktop. These posts often show up on a website called Reddit, where anonymous users suffer no consequences after shaming the original content producer (ex. your kid) by posting the screenshots of their content, like a tweet. A photo posted can also turn into a "meme"—a virus-like photo with a funny caption that spreads throughout the internet like wildfire. Once something makes it to Reddit, there is a good chance that it will spread to Facebook and elsewhere. Some people, like Justine Sacco, with less than 200 followers on Twitter, have found their content spread to hundreds of thousands of people within an hour. There's just no way to get that content back.

4. **Bloggers.** Anything posted online that offends certain communities is sure to be blogged about right away. Bloggers are rewarded for having fresh content that is controversial.

Social media posts are like digital tattoos. Getting a face tattoo might be a good decision for the lead singer of a punk band, creating visibility and credibility in punk communities, leading to great success as a punk artist. But if that person wants to be an elementary school teacher, a court judge, a nurse later in life, that face tattoo could be a major life handicap, shouting, "I don't fit in with this community! You won't relate to me!"

We are branding ourselves all the time with how we dress, how we talk, how we look. Which isn't to say that we can judge everything about someone based on how they look or by one thing they've said. Rather, how we brand ourselves is like a shorthand communication to send signals to other people in communities we want to be a part of that we have shared interests and goals.

How you brand yourself on the internet can affect the rest of your life. Your digital tattoos are seen by colleges and employers from their point of view, without the back story or rationale. Make sure that your kid's digital tattoo is unambiguously positive or at least neutral so that they don't limit their options now or later in life, keeping their self-branding options open.

Right now, your child may be 13 or 14, or even younger, if you want a head start (which is great, since it's never too early to care about their online image). Their big goals are probably getting on a sport's team, a school club, and in the near future, getting into college. But what about after that? Getting into college isn't the last step. What does your child want to do after that? In the next 10 years, they're going to want to join their favorite college club or sports team, get a life-changing internship, travel with a study abroad program, get a part-time job to pay for college, get into a graduate program, finally graduate college, get a real-world job, enter public service, etc. All of these are great ambitions,

> *Productivity is never an accident. It is always the result of commitment to excellence, intelligent planning, and focused effort.*
> - Paul J. Meyer

but 50% of their posts could possibly hinder them from some of these goals.

Your social media reputation doesn't start when you get online; it starts when your friends get online. Parents are saying, "My son Billy is 12 years old and we don't let him have a phone, so he has no online footprint. His reputation is totally clean." Actually, if Billy's friends are uploading and posting photos of him at events and trying to tag him in them (even when the photos aren't the most flattering), his reputation has already started. Between friends, this is fun. But putting things online takes it out of the realm of friendship and lets anyone see it and form an opinion about it. Tell your child that they need to be careful what they put online and what they let other people put online about them.

Indecision and delays are the parents of failure.
- George Canning

Visit SafeSmartSocial.com/book to register this book for free and we will send you videos and key takeaways to help your students use social media to impress colleges and employers.

Key takeaways from this chapter:

- Even people with few followers can find their poorly planned tweets being shared and discussed widely on social media and then news organizations.
- You're only as good as your ten most recent posts.
- The SOK—Silent Opportunity Killer—can be responsible for lost opportunities, without you ever being aware.
- Even distracting content can be an SOK. It might seem innocuous, but if it doesn't further a person's goals, it detracts.
- The Internet Archive, Google's caches, screenshots saved and replicated elsewhere outside of your control, and bloggers are the top reasons for why

content doesn't usually disappear.

- You are branding yourself all the time, whether you like it or realize it. Make sure that the branding you choose reflects who you are and are striving to be, and will work for the next five years.
- Your kid's social media reputation starts when their friends get online.

CHAPTER TWO

Common social media mistakes made

Born and raised in Ireland, I moved to Australia for two years on a working holiday visa. I returned to Ireland for one year to figure out what I wanted to do for my career. I then applied for a six month holiday visa back to Australia to live with friends until I figured out what I wanted to do. Keep in mind, this wasn't a work visa, just a holiday visa.

After traveling for 24 hours from Ireland to Australia, I was pretty tired. As I was going through immigration the Australian airport officials suddenly stopped me and asked me for more details. They wanted to know why I was visiting, why I don't have return flights and what I was going to do while I was here on a non-work holiday. I explained that I might go to New Zealand during the six months I was there. After giving them all my visa paperwork, the officials called me over to a computer with a web browser set to Facebook.com on the screen. The woman told me to put in my details. I was thinking, "There's no way they can snoop through all my private messages," but they did. Straight away there was a conversation between myself and a friend... she was asking what my plans were in Australia and I explained,

"I'm not sure. I just need a break but I might try to find a job."

Straight away the immigration officials highlighted this. The officials had already confiscated my phone and they proceeded to lookup the name of the person meeting me at the airport and told her to go home, since I wouldn't be leaving anytime soon. I wasn't aware this was happening.

I was brought into a room and interviewed for about four hours waiting to hear their decision. They decided to cancel my visa and slap me with a three-year ban! I am not allowed to visit Australia for three years!

I was then given a bright orange jacket and escorted out the back entrance of the airport into a bus and brought to a detention center where I had to remain until they could contact my airline to organize my flight home.

When I arrived they searched my bags and all I was allowed to keep was pj's and underwear and was given a card with $20 on it to spend in the detention 'shop.'
I spent two nights in the detention center which had four Irish lads each with their own crazy stories. The next morning I awoke to an English girl in my "cell" sitting next to me who looked at me and said, "You also in here because of Facebook?"

Some people were, in there for stabbings and other assaults, we were put in the same cell.

My best bet was to fly to China. So off I went to Guangzhou International Airport and after landing I quickly realized they weren't allowing me to exit the plane. They gave me no explanation, but after 1.5 hours they allowed me to deplane and then they told me I wasn't welcome there. China heard that Australia didn't want me and they were basically kicking me out without even letting me

Experience is simply the name we give our mistakes.
- Oscar Wilde

visit. I told them I'm going to Bali so we verbally agreed I cannot return to China (I still have no idea what actually happened there but after 11 hours in that airport it was not fun). They kept my passport and luggage up to one hour before I boarded the flight from China to Bali."

This is an unusual story from Lisa Coghlan, a friend of a friend. While this kind of situation may not happen a lot, it's a dramatic enough story to hopefully stick in your memory, acting as an emotional mnemonic-type device that will cause you to remember the need to be careful and mindful in social media activities. Because, according to Jobvite.com, 93% of recruiters check social media activities. Kaplan reports that up to 30% of college recruiters are doing the same. It's time to clean up our act before it becomes the norm for recruiters to want to be friended on social media!

So, now that you've thought about what your kids want to accomplish in the years to come, what would a disappointment look like? Would it be working four long years through advanced classes in high school, participating in community service and extracurricular activities, saving for college, only to be denied their school of choice? Not because of their GPA, but because of an errant Facebook post that comes across to some as risqué? "That's not fair!" you say. Maybe not. "People are not robots. They deserve to be seen as individuals, with flaws as well as strengths!" you say. Maybe so. But it's just the way people are when they have something they consider to be valuable and they have to decide with whom they will share it.

At the end of the day, the most overwhelming key to a child's success is the positive involvement of parents.
– Jane D. Hull

It's like dating. If you were dating again, particularly online, would you want to learn everything about someone right away, including what they are like when they are angry and depressed? Would you want to see photos of them in their pajamas with messed up hair and smell their morning breath? Most people would say no, because they want to be romanced and be introduced to their partner's darker side while they're wearing love goggles. They know that no one is perfect, but that honeymoon period is so brief that they want to enjoy it while they can. We want to be charmed. If you found two online dating profiles which were almost identical in all positive aspects but one of them also shared damning details, you would most likely gravitate toward the shiny, flawless profile, on the chance that people really are out there who are just that great.

> *In this life, we have to make many choices. The choices we make determine to a large extent our happiness or our unhappiness, because we have to live with the consequences of our choices.*
> – James E. Faust

This is what admissions officers do every day. You don't need to agree with it, but you do need to accept that it happens and understand why.

Here are some possible scenarios for college applicants:

Crass content

Christina, a 17-year-old high school junior applying for college, posts positive quotes on social media, fun pictures of friends, and retweets fun celeb tweets. Generally she isn't dramatic or negative on social media, so she thinks she's doing well. However, one day she's watching The Bachelor TV show and, heated in the moment when her favorite contestant gets kicked off, she tweets, "Why did Rebecca get picked over Susan? Susan is such a slut! #bachelor." This one tweet is going to be the message that her college admissions officers might take note of when they are looking at her application and they search her name online. They might wonder, Is this applicant a bully? Does she stir up drama? Is she competitive and non-supportive to women whose values differ from hers?

Does she too strongly identify with a tribe, to the point of being exclusionary?

Disingenuous and politically incorrect content

Justin, an 18-year-old senior applying for scholarships, posts photos on Instagram of himself with his grandmother, helping his nephews learn to read, and playing football. He shares inspirational quotes on Twitter about helping others, about thinking positively, and showing empathy. He seems like a stand-out kid, with unusually mature understanding. Then someone stumbles upon some online comment of his stating that, "Bums just leech off the system. Get a job." This single comment will cause him to appear a phony, even if he was sincere in all of his positive posts, and unaware that it's not politically correct to refer to homeless people by a word that makes them sound like something other than people. The term for this is "othering," and universities are cracking down on othering language, as they try to create more inclusive environments. If Justin doesn't see the value of lending a hand to less fortunate people, why should he be deserving of free money through a scholarship?

Silly and distracting content

Britney is a 16-year-old whiz kid applying to Harvard already. Her grades are incredible, she's won national science awards, and she volunteers at her local animal shelter. She knows that she is ahead of most of her peers in terms of candidacy, so she doesn't put much care into her online reputation. She posts frequent selfies on Instagram making silly faces and her Tumblr account has a notable percentage of reblogs of photos of kittens wearing clothes. She's sixteen, applying to university early. Her grades are impressive but will she be able to fit in? admissions advisors wonder. If she was 18, advisors might think, "She doesn't look very serious. It looks like everything comes to her easily. She might not apply herself studiously to our rigorous programs."

By now, you should be starting to see how easy it is for

your kid to blow this great opportunity to showcase themselves in a way that is positive, authentic, and aligned with how they are marketing themselves to college admissions employees ready to evaluate them.

But being forward thinking shouldn't stop there. Before we discuss specifics of what not to do, followed by what to do, I want to further drive home for you just how problematic social media run amok can be. Check out the following examples of how to make your life unnecessarily difficult using social media.

How high school party pics can lose a college sporting scholarship

When Eden Prairie High School cracked down on students posting pictures of underage drinking to social media accounts, nearly 100 students were brought to the principal and questioned or reprimanded about the online photos that showed them partying, drinking, and the like. While some students denied that they actually were drinking, the ambiguity was enough to get them in trouble, and in some cases expelled or suspended. Some of the students lost scholarship opportunities since they were dropped from sports teams during their senior year and were not able to perform in front of college recruiters.[1]

> *If you live long enough, you'll make mistakes. But if you learn from them, you'll be a better person. It's how you handle adversity, not how it affects you. The main thing is never quit, never quit, never quit.*
> -William J. Clinton

Tactical Tip: If you show up to a party where there's something happening that's illegal (or makes you uncomfortable) leave the party ASAP. Even if you don't drink, you may be tagged in photos (or checked in online with other

---

1. Emily Friedman, "Minn. High Schoolers Suspended for Facebook Pics," *ABCNews.com*, last modified January 10, 2008, SafeSmartSocial.com/research.

people) and that will bring you into the principal's office to be questioned with the other students. It's ok to have fun, but the best policy is to stay away from any drinking parties, and to not give others the opportunity to take pictures of you in situations like this.

How to lose a college acceptance

As reported in *The New York Times* in 2013, a prospective student was attending an informational session at Bowdoin College in Brunswick, ME. To the admission officers' great surprise, that student was posting rude, degrading comments about her fellow prospects to her Twitter account. Since the officers monitored their Twitter mentions, the student's remarks were easily found. She was denied admission (based on her grades), but the administrators said that those posts would have hindered her chances, had she been more competitive. They were baffled by the judgment of someone who would so openly make hateful remarks.[2]

> It's fine to celebrate success but it is more important to heed the lessons of failure.
> – Bill Gates

Tactical Tip: Everything you say online is your public diary. Take care before you say anything negative or hurtful since it can all be found with one search and you could lose out on a great opportunity.

How to get fired before you start your new job

Recently a young woman was offered a job at Cisco. Cisco has over 70,000 employees and offices on 5+ continents. This would be a dream job for most young professionals. Immediately after receiving the offer, what do you think she did? She went to Twitter and posted: "Cisco just offered me a job! Now I have to weigh the fatty paycheck against the daily

---

2. Natasha Singer, "They Loved Your GPA Then They Saw Your Tweets," *The New York Times*, last modified November 9, 2013, SafeSmartSocial.com/research.

commute and hating the work."[3]

Do you think Cisco listens to their brand online? Of course, especially since their high tech products need fast paced customer service and the sales team always likes knowing what happens in the field. Do you think Cisco listens to their brand on Twitter even when you don't include the "@" sign before their name? You guessed it, yes. They are always listening to provide the best customer service. Most companies do this.

The best way of removing negativity is to laugh and be joyous.

– David Icke

Shortly after the job candidate sent the tweet, a senior level employee at Cisco found this post and responded on Twitter with: "Who is the hiring manager? I'm sure they would love to know that you will hate the work. We here at Cisco are versed in the Web."

Of course, she was fired before she even started working at the company. Her tweet ruined her chances of having a great career at a global corporation. She received notice from the HR department that her offer was rescinded and that she didn't need to report to work. Sadly, this story is all over the web. Major news outlets picked up the tweets and reported it on their sites. This young job candidate's name is all over the web when you search for "Cisco Fatty Paycheck."

Tactical Tip: If you are accepted to a job (or college), consider only calling your close friends and not announcing it via social media. Once you get your first week (or month) under your belt in your new role, then take a classy group photo thanking your new college/employer for the chance to be a part of their new family.

How to get fired releasing company secrets on Twitter

---

3. Helen A.S. Popkin, "Twitter Gets You Fired in 140 Characters or Less," *Technotica.com*, last modified March 23, 2009, SafeSmartSocial.com/research.

A young woman who got her big break to be featured in the TV show GLEE thought it would be fun to release secret information. She used her Twitter profile to announce spoiler info before new TV show episodes were aired. She found out that she was fired when her producer/boss replied promptly by Tweeting: "Hope you're qualified to do something besides work in entertainment." When she announced this information she was leaking company secrets without thinking what was in the best interest of her employer (or her career).[4]

Tactical Tip: If you ever want to talk badly about a company or person, consider calling someone instead of posting it online.

How to get fired with offensive remarks

Famous comedian Gilbert Gottfried got in trouble for making an insensitive joke about the Japanese tsunami, which got him fired from his job as the voice of the Aflac duck. His tweet read, "I just split up with my girlfriend, but like the Japanese say, 'They'll be another one floating by any minute now.'" This goes to show that even the famous, who are paid to make off-color jokes, can get in trouble for being careless.[5]

Tactical Tip: When you try to be funny, there will probably be someone of whom you're making fun. Consider using self-deprecating humor (and point fun at yourself first), so you can make others laugh at your expense, and generally have less of a chance of upsetting someone. Also, consider rereading all of your tweets twice and asking yourself, "How

---

4. Nardine Saad, "Glee Spoiler Extra Fired Nicole Crowther," The Gospel on Celebrity Pop Culture, *Los Angeles Times*, last modified April 21, 2011, SafeSmartSocial.com/research.

5. "Gilbert Gottfried Fired As Aflac Duck After Tweet About Japanese Tsunami," *Huffington Post Entertainment*, last modified May 25, 2011, SafeSmartSocial.com/research.

can this go wrong?"

How to get fired by ignoring safety practices

A few Dominos employees thought it would be funny to take a video of them doing gross things to food at work. They later uploaded it to YouTube to show to friends. That food was probably served to customers, which painted the company in a very bad light and certainly cost them at least a few patrons when the video was discovered for everyone to see. The employees had no idea their small video would be discovered by the whole word (let alone their employer) and they quickly lost their jobs.[6]

Tactical Tip: Everything you post on social media could easily be seen by your current (and future) employers. Make sure you're living a life at work that's Light, Bright and Polite® so everything you do will make your employer proud. It's OK to make honest mistakes at work, but thinking you'll get away with something funny on social media will come back to haunt you. Ask yourself before you post, "When my boss sees this, will they be proud of my work?"

How to lose a court battle with one Tweet

Prep school graduate Dana cost her dad $80,000 by sharing confidential information on Facebook. Her father was in a lawsuit with the prep school that she attended and had won $10,000 in back wages and an $80,000 settlement, as long as the details were kept confidential. Without thinking, Dana thought it would be funny to post to her Facebook account, "Mama and Papa won the case against my school. They are now officially paying for my vacation to Europe this summer. SUCK IT."

Tactical Tip: Being silent on social media during an

---

6. "Domino's Workers Disgusting YouTube Video: Spitting, Nose-Picking and Worse," *Huffington Post*, last modified May 25, 2011, SafeSmartSocial.com/research.

important life event can be a very wise decision. Certainly, going through the settlement was trying and stressful for her family. It's reasonable to be happy that something good came out of the tough situation. However, by announcing anything important to social media, we jeopardize having a chance of a favorable outcome, for ourselves and others.

How to get your parents robbed

In 2012, a teenage girl took a picture of her grandmother's cash savings, while she was helping her grandmother count out the money. She posted that picture to Facebook, which garnered her some unwanted attention. The same day, later in the evening, two armed robbers showed up at the girl's parent's house, some 75 miles away from where she was living at the time and robbed the family.

The girl's careless post could have cost her parents a lot more, though. When the robbers arrived at the house, they demanded to speak to the girl from the Facebook post. Her parents had to tell them that she no longer lived there. Any number of things could have happened – from them getting angry to hurting to family. Luckily only a small amount of cash and personal belongings were taken and no one was hurt.[7]

Tactical Tip: Don't brag online. If something seems really impressive, take a photo of it and show your parents, and/or friends via text message. Don't post photos of cash, jewelry, big screen TVs or anything valuable. You're making yourself a target so someone can find out where you live and you will garner unwanted attention.

These are some dramatic situations you may have read about in the news. "Sure," you may say. "These were pretty

---

7. Mike Flacy, "Teenage Girl Posts Picture of Cash on Facebook, Family Robbed Within Hours," *DigitalTrends.com*, last modified May 29, 2011, SafeSmartSocial.com/research.

thoughtless decisions. I or my kid wouldn't do anything so reckless or irresponsible." Hopefully not.

But there's more to it than that. Here is another sample list of items that both you and your child might consider avoiding on social media:

- Political opinions or viewpoints
- Breakups or relationship problems
- Mushy love stories that might make others cringe
- Frustrated moments at the bank/grocery store/traffic
- Photos of you with friends or significant others out drinking

This is how these misguided social media posts can appear:

Political Views

"I can't believe that politician voted for that bill. They obviously hate minorities."

Appearance: As a former candidate myself, I know that each issue has a lot of moving parts. When using a blanket statement like this you seem insensitive, uniformed and unable to see nuance. Even if others in the political system comment like this, try to avoid joining them. A post like this says to the world: "I haven't done all my research and I'm going to side with the first person who told me their side of the issue."

Boss Complaints

"My boss is an idiot. Am I the only one that understands what goes on around here?"

Appearance: There's a good chance your future employer (or current boss) will see this post. Since many of your friends will help you find your future job, you're telling your friends: "I'm dramatic and if you invite me to interview at your company, I'll talk this way about your boss and get us both in trouble." Also, assume that your current boss can see everything you are posting on social media.

TV Show Trash Talking

"Rebecca didn't get a rose tonight on The Bachelor. Ha, karma is a b*tch for what she said on last week's episode!"

Appearance: This might be a great text message to a friend (or comment on the couch), but it says to a college/employer: "I'm going to be distasteful and kick people while they are down." Instead, consider saying something that doesn't seem to revel in someone else's pain. Or just save your offhanded, emotional remark for a text to a friend.

Dating/Single Life

"Online dating sucks! Aren't there any decent guys out there?"

Appearance: Dating is never easy. However, this says to the world, "I'm frustrated and I'm looking for attention." If a future date googles you, do you think this is something they will be attracted to? Perhaps they would want to see something more positive describing an outlook or trait that you admire in someone else.

Trash Talking a Referee

"That call was BS! That should have been a touchdown for UCLA! These refs suck!"

Appearance: Good sportsmanlike conduct happens both on the field and online. If you complain about things not going your way you are saying to the world: "I'm going to trash talk anyone that I disagree with and share it publicly. Don't invite me on your team or to work at your company."

Traffic Congestion

"People in this city can't drive. One accident stopped the whole freeway and all I wanted to do was get home to relax after a long day's work."

Appearance: We all get frustrated and traffic doesn't help the situation. However, consider being more sensitive when a post involves outside circumstances. This post says to the world: "Although someone may have been critically injured in an auto accident, I'm still going to only see the world from my standpoint and be frustrated (instead of thankful that it wasn't me)."

Religion

(I'm going to avoid an example altogether so as not to offend anyone.)

Appearance: Try to avoid any negative posts about someone's beliefs in a higher power. It will never get you anywhere closer to making friends if it's opinionated, or it will have you making only friends who are just like you, which limits your ability to advance in the world and work with varieties of people.

Sharing time-sensitive info publicly (instead of with your family/friends)

"For those of you who know me, tomorrow I have a first round interview at XYZ Company. Many of you know that this is a big deal for me and I don't know what I'll do if I don't get the offer."

Appearance: This might be a great conversation to share with your family and/or friends, however, there's a good chance the future employer is going to see this post also. It may be a better idea to wait until after you hear back from the employer to announce your new job (or wait a month to tell people how much you love it). If you stack all of your emotions into one post it says to the world: "I'm needy and I haven't thought this through all the way. I might be a little unstable or dramatic if this doesn't go exactly as planned."

Don't share your relationship drama

"What is it with people who never replace the toilet paper on the roll? They're always the same people who squeeze from the middle of the toothpaste tube!"

Appearance: Next, if you are in a wonderful relationship, that's great. Keep it clean online. Post some Light, Bright, and Polite® group pictures of you going to events or dates together. If you are not in a wonderful relationship, or a relationship at all, don't fall into the trap of posting how annoying it is to see people's baby pictures and how you're so tired of people asking you, "Why aren't you married?" Not only will employers see these posts, but also your kids will see them and it will send a message that it's ok to post content about your relationships to get public feedback from friends. You could use the same opportunity to post positive things about what you are doing, not negative things about other people. If you are single, unhappy, or looking for love, social media is perhaps not the place to share your thoughts on the subject.

It would seem like there are a lot of rules of what not to do! Wouldn't it be easier if there were some general rules to keep in mind, some categories of things to keep in mind?

We went to our friends at BrandYourself.com for some advice. They guided us to segment potential problems into four categories. We have modified them to work with teens and tweens:

Positive and on topic with your resume/application (Light, Bright, and Polite®)

These Google results should give people confidence they have found the person for whom they are searching. These results should highlight your full name, include a clear set of photos of you volunteering (or working on school projects) and they all tell a story that is very similar to your resume. The goal here is to have colleges discover that your online results are a three dimensional version of your printed resume/application. If you are applying for a musical scholarship, they should discover your YouTube account on the first page of Google with several videos that highlight your performances (and maybe a couple that teach others how to play an instrument).

If your resume says you were captain of the football team, your online results should carefully resemble this with relevant photos and links. If a college/employer clicks the "images" button on Google they should see a vibrant set of images that include your volunteer projects, extracurricular activities and a positive social media footprint that blends well with their culture. They should not find any careless photos of you, but rather a carefully crafted quilt of images that show them a slice of your work ethic, your smile and your productive pastime.   encourage, congratulate, and highlight the accomplishments of other people. They should never speak negatively or casually joke about topics surrounding race, culture, ethnicity, sex or gender identity, disability or inability, sexual orientation, creed/religion, age, economic class or educational level, political affiliation, or style.

It should be enough to just say, "Be kind and polite!" but sometimes people feel like it's just silly good fun to make a casual remark about someone's clothes or race or culture. It's good to be aware of why these comments are considered so hurtful and offensive, and if in doubt, don't post!

Party mode (red cups)

Photos depicting alcohol consumption, especially underage, raises red flags for a lot of employers and colleges. Even if it's Coke in a red cup, the appearance is that you like to party. You might be a very wholesome person in real life, never holding a red cup or drinking alcohol underage, however, if you spend a lot of time with those that do party, your Google results will blend with theirs. If your real life friends have red cups and you get tagged in their photos, you will be put into the "party stack" of resumes. A few of these photos sprinkled throughout a social media profile (or Google image search) strongly indicates partying as a favorite past time, instead of, say, volunteering or entrepreneuring. But even one photo can appear to have snuck through accidentally, causing the evaluator to wonder if this one photo is foreboding of potential problems.

Silly & off topic (selfies)

Your kid could have the highest grades in their class,

but if someone searches for them and finds a high percentage of photos from pie-eating contests, backyard BBQs and harmless tailgating at sporting events, it will distract from the overall impression they are trying to create of someone who is studious, productive, innovative, charitable, actively engaged in community improvement. If many of these photos are selfies, it may leave the evaluator with a sense that your child doesn't volunteer (and that they are narcissistic).

Who are those people? (AKA: Doppelgangers who have the same name but aren't your kid)

If you search for your kid and other people show up in the search results, this could be dangerous territory to be in because you have no control over the kind of online reputation these other random individuals may have. If they look similar to your kid or live in the same city, colleges and employers could get confused and conflate both people. Whether they were awarded a hero award for rescuing a drowning child or they were arrested for abusing animals, you don't want your kid to get mixed up with them. You want your kid accurately evaluated for what they can contribute. Or maybe it's clear that these other people are different, because they live in another state, but they are still hogging search results for being famous or infamous. If this is the case, the person evaluating your kid could just give up before getting a chance to be impressed (or, more likely, they will become frustrated that your kid isn't easy to find, which will give them a negative impression). We don't want this! It's considered a savvy skill to manage one's Google search results, to create a positive reputation.

In addition, we'd like to add and emphasize:

Tag, you're it!

It's important to be aware of who is tagging your child in photos and for what. If a friend of theirs played a prank on someone and tagged a bunch of their friends in a photo of the prank so they would all see it and comment, an advisor or evaluator coming across this post may not realize that your child tagged in the photo was not a part of the prank itself.

Avoid political topics

This could fit into being Light, Bright and Polite® but it deserves emphasis. Here's the thing: Because the country is divided right down the middle on most issues, make sure that your kid considers the risk of sharing any political viewpoints anywhere on social media. And that you consider the risk of doing this yourself: If you talk politics on your Facebook page, your kids are going to feel more comfortable sharing their own controversial opinions to their online friends. Chances are, if they are a Democrat, the job they're applying to may have a Republican boss. It doesn't matter what side you're on, you have almost a 50/50 chance of being on the opposite camp of the person you or your child is trying to impress. Most people never keep this in mind when they post on social media.

> *Computers and the Internet have made it really easy to rant. It's made everyone overly opinionated.*
> – Scott Weiland

Most people, when discussing politics, become super passionate and even defensive in their view point. Naturally, no one wants to feel their world view is wrong. Since political rants can reflect some of our deepest held opinions, they are not always conducted in a rational manner. Typically they are missing a two-way communication about the facts. Political rants can also come across as very negative, especially when you feel strongly about a topic in the public eye. Your kid may be planning a career in writing or politics where knowledge, interest and even passion in these topics is important to exhibit for credibility and to make a name for one's self. If this is the case, it's still a good idea to be extra conscientious to not appear to be single-minded, angry, and condescending as many people can tend to become when arguing about ideas they hold most dear.

If your kid shows that they see both sides, shows some

thoughtfulness and empathy toward opposing ideas, which are, remember, coming from other people, that can cause them to stand out as uniquely intelligent and kind. But this is hard for people to do well, and even more hard for younger, passionate people who are more prone to being black-and-white thinkers. So, just keep in mind your ultimate goal here: To get into your school of choice/internship/job. And remember that since about half of the country feels differently than you do, depending on where you live, there's a great chance of offending 50% of the people out there.

The worst is if you write a political rant that says, "I can't believe this politician wants to suppress people... everyone that voted this way must be evil..." And yet someone else, whether they're right or wrong, disagrees with you, you have created a silent opportunity killer (SOK).

An SOK is the same as carrying around a sign that says, "I have a dramatic cloud over my head, please move out of the way." Do you think your friends or future employer will comment on your posts,

> *Children learn to smile from their parents.*
> -Shinichi Suzuki

looking for more information about why you feel so strongly, trying to see your point of view? No, they will simply take a mental note that you are willing to share your personal opinion on your social media accounts for all to see (and many times that opinion is somewhat close-minded). For every person who agrees with you on politics, chances are there are at least two who are offended and taking note of your stance. Sometimes, even people on your same side of the issue can notice how dramatic you are in your "argument" and avoid commenting because it may drag them down and make them look careless in their online brand.

These are things for your kids to watch out for. But you, too, parents can negatively affect your kids' chances.

Parents need to consider not commenting on their kids' posts.

If you become friends with your kids, please consider merely reading their posts and giving them some space online. Not only could your own ill-advised comment affect their opportunities, they also just need space to not feel smothered. Making a child feel smothered online will probably embarrass them and they will work hard to hide their online activities from you. 'Don't kill the golden goose.' Instead, try not commenting on most of their posts. The best way to maintain your online friendship connection with your kids on each specific network is to not smother them. Just like in real life, you give your kids space to run around, all while observing from a distance to make sure that they don't get hurt. Let them play and have fun, while allowing them to feel like they could come back to you at any moment. Social media should be treated in a similar fashion.

Visit SafeSmartSocial.com/book to register this book for free and we will send you videos and key takeaways to help your students use social media to impress colleges and employers.

Key takeaways from this chapter:

- Officials can ask to see your social media content. The fall-out can be huge.
- Do not share posts that are complaining, religious, trash-talking or relationship drama.
- Keep posts positive, on-topic, and kind. Avoid anything risqué or politically incorrect to make a joke.
- Educate yourself on what is considered politically incorrect these days.
- No party photos! Kids are writing their resumes one red cup at a time.
- Avoid silly and distracting content.
- Be aware of being tagged in photos, set up your accounts so that tags have to be approved, and remove or ask others to remove tags you don't want.

- Avoid political commentary. It's hard to do this well in a way that doesn't alienate others. Best to just avoid it, if possible.
- Create a recognizable profile for yourself online so that you aren't mistake for your doppelgangers.
- If your kid is reaching out on social media in ways that affect their reputation, giving the impression of neediness or drama craving, introduce them to new ways of reaching out and getting help. Several good resources exist. They just need better tools.

CHAPTER THREE
Social media strategies and posts that impress colleges

At the end of the day, the most overwhelming key to a child's success is the positive involvement of parents. – Jane D. Hull

---

I n May of 2009, I ran for city council of Hermosa Beach, a small beach community in Los Angeles. My decision to run was not an easy one. Initially, I was relatively unknown by community leaders. I was up against eight-year incumbents and candidates with experience in three past races, who were all pretty well known. But, I set out to knock on 3,015 doors, meeting voters at their homes so they could know me as well as they knew the competition.

During my campaign, a close friend phoned asking, "Did you see what someone wrote about you online?" I quickly googled myself but couldn't find anything negative. I asked my friend how they found the info. After a bit of puzzlement, I discovered that my friends (and perhaps local voters) saw a very different version of Google results than I did. They could easily find negative press about me on their first page of Google. I had to scroll through about five pages to see the same negative results my friends were talking about: blog posts written by two local residents.

Realizing they had never met me, I strongly believed these bloggers would respect my hard work and change their opinion about me when they learned that I had the community's best interest at heart. I emailed them both, asking if they would meet me for coffee in the next few days to sit down and talk about the issues but they wouldn't respond or meet.

I had every right to feel indignant, unfairly maligned and defensive when one of the bloggers attended to the city council debate and targeted me with a question given in a scathing tone, meant to throw me off guard. Instead, I began, "Hello, how are you tonight?" I treated her like she was the only vote in the room, genuinely taking interest in her question and her concern. I answered with poise, was kind and did my best to make sure she was pleased with my response. Unfortunately, nothing I said changed her opinion that night. By the look on her face, she was set on making me squirm on stage. It seemed like a failed exchange.

However, at the end of the debate, a nice woman approached and said, "Hi Josh. I wasn't going to vote for you yesterday, but now I am." I thanked her and asked why. She replied, "None of us like that woman who asked you the mean question in the debate. In fact, we all know how she behaves and we don't agree with most of what she says. However, you were so gracious with her that we learned more about you than we could have otherwise. We learned that you are nice and courteous to those who are mean to you. You have my vote, and the votes of many of my friends in the back of the room."

Social media creates many opportunities for these kinds of aggressive, antagonistic exchanges, especially when people do not have to see the impact of their words upon the faces of the people they address online. For younger people with less life experience, it's even easier for them to not understand the impact of their words. Even if they were able to see the faces of the people they talk to on Tumblr and Twitter, they may not understand what those facial expressions mean, because they haven't experienced either hurting people or being hurt often enough to realize the impact they are having on others. It's too easy to be rude. Even when we aren't being rude, the lack of intonation and body language with online writing can lead people to think we are.

Most people will encounter opportunities online to lose their cool, to give in to temptation to try a risky joke, share a compromising photo, or engage in conflict. Staying Light, Bright and Polite® when it would be understandable if we weren't, is to be remarkable, and therefore memorable.

So, what does an ace social media game look like?

Kim Sanchez, former Director of Online Safety & Accessibility at Microsoft has a few tips for taking charge of your online reputation. She says,

1. **Protect your online reputation.** Act online in a manner that reflects the reputation you want to earn. Don't trick yourself into feeling like offline and online are separate worlds. They co-mingle and a reputation in one world can alter one's reputation in the other.
2. **Think before you share.** Think about what you are posting (particularly suggestive photos and videos), with whom you are sharing the information, and how it will reflect on your reputation. Don't post when drinking, when sad or angry.
3. **Treat others as you would like to be treated.** Respect the reputation and privacy of others when you post anything about them (including pictures).
4. **Consider whether you want your profiles to be public or more private.** Look for Settings or Options to help you manage who can see your profile or photos, how people can search for you, who can comment, and how to block unwanted access.
5. **Periodically reassess who has access to your pages.** It's okay to remove those who no longer belong.

People are vulnerable to negativity bias. We can be rays of sunshine, thoroughly Light, Bright and Polite® every day

For every minute you are angry you lose sixty seconds of happiness.
– Ralph Waldo Emerson

for months, until one day we engage in an angry exchange on social media. Maybe this only happens once or twice ever, but guess what people remember? We only remember the truly remarkable. So, **even if you are a great person, posting great content on a regular basis, it may not be what people remember about you if you are prone to the occasional outburst or insensitive remark. Take a five minute break before posting a frustrated comment.**

Like kids, many parents vent their anger online. They're under a lot of stress, so they need to share with someone, and expressing their frustrations online is the easiest place to get a quick response. Instead of sharing frustrated posts online, parents should consider using the five minute rule. First, open a new email in your browser (or on your phone). Don't insert any email addresses in the "TO:" section. Then, write out your anger as if you were letting it all out with your best friend. Don't be shy, say what's on your mind and use any words that make you feel better (sometimes these might not be so Light, Bright or Polite®). Thankfully, you can't accidentally send this email to someone since it isn't addressed to anyone, so you can feel more comfortable sharing how angry, upset or hurt you are about the situation. Then, title the email with a fitting subject and save it to draft mode. Walk away from the computer (or put down your phone) and go do something else for at least five minutes.

The best time for yout to hold your tongue is the time you feel you must say something or bust.
-Josh Billings

Then, five minutes later, reread the email and ask yourself if you're still upset. If you're not upset, save the draft for future reference and move on. However, if you're still passionate about the email, decide who you could call (or text) to explain the situation. This should be someone that you're really close to and trust not to tell anyone about it.

I use this technique every month when I'm frustrated with someone in business. The more I use it, the happier I tend to be. It's a great way to put your frustrations "on paper" without having them hurt your reputation (or someone else's).

More often than not, this draft is going to let you vent the anger to yourself, without needing to vent it to that person. After a few minutes, you'll have a chance to see the full picture. Why did they do that? Did they know it would hurt you? Maybe it seemed like the best thing for them to do at the time. Maybe it had nothing to do with you. Maybe there are parts of the story that you should ask for before getting so mad.

If you do need to confront that person, "start with the heart." Introduced to me in the book *Crucial Conversations* (McGraw-Hill), I regularly encourage people to use it by saying, "I want to have a conversation about how that made me feel." You can go on by emphasizing with that person. "I understand that this is where you were coming from...and I appreciate all that you do on a regular basis." I like to make sure that I explain my side in a calm and rational manner (not always very easy to do). Here's an example: "Perhaps you didn't mean to make me feel that way, but this is how I felt as a result." Then explain the facts that led you to feel that way. Then, ask them, "Do you think my feelings are a fair representation for that situation?" Finish with trying to empathize with them, and then reiterate the inputs that led you to be upset. You can then talk about the bigger picture. This is my favorite line to talk about when referencing the

> *I've learned that people will forget what you said, people will forget what you did, but people will never forget how you made them feel.*
> – Maya Angelou

bigger picture: "…We're going to be friends for a very long time after this, I just wanted to let you know how that made me feel so that we can stay focused on the future, and not have any misunderstandings between us."

I'm often sensitive to other people's actions towards me. If someone says something that affects me, I can sometimes beat myself up on the inside for several hours as I assume the worst. Approaching people quickly and "starting with heart" helps me open up a line of communication between that person and quickly resolves the issue (not to mention it makes me feel much better). Also, this has kept my social media accounts very clean and helps me to not hurt any of my friendships by reacting impulsively. Most of the time when I have this talk with someone, I quickly realize I had totally misunderstood them and we quickly get on the right page together.

> *Correction does much, but encouragement does more.*
> -Johann Wolfgang von Goethe

Here's Facebook's advice on posting hurtful content:

It's easy to get caught up in the moment and write or do something that may seem hilarious at the time. But remember, what you say can really hurt someone, or come back to haunt you. Think before you post. It only takes a second or two. Ask yourself if you really want to say it. Make sure you don't mind if your friends, classmates, or teachers hear about it later.

Dale Carnegie, in his book *How to Win Friends and Influence People* describes a way to connect with others (and save time and irritation) by asking yourself this one simple question before getting upset: "How would I feel, how would I react if I were in [that person's] shoes?" – Dale Carnegie

I find myself saying this quote in my head at least once

a week. It helps me to step back and give me a new perspective so I can talk with that person in a calm manner that helps me to better appreciate that person. Even if you say to yourself, "I might not understand where they're coming from, they may have had a tough day," it could be enough to calm you down.

For parents and kids, it's never a good idea to tweet or respond online in a heated manner that could be viewed in a way that's anything other than Light, Bright and Polite®. Especially if you are angry or in a rush.

Before you hit the submit button, make sure that your post is something you can call your Grandma about and tell her over the phone. There are a lot of examples of people who have posted something while they were upset, flustered or they thought it was "funny" but it came back to bite them.

Jim Ellis, Dean of the USC Marshall School of Business gives the following four pieces of advice to new college students:

Use social media in a positive manner. When you complain online or post in a dramatic way, you walk around with a black cloud over your head on social media that others can follow. Be thoughtful in the messages you post/send.

Be a positive thought leader in something. Use social media to your advantage to build your name/image online. Being a thought leader means taking something that you are already good at and sharing it with other people so that you can help them be good at it too.

Don't permanentize things. Every time you put things in writing you permanentize your actions. Anything that goes on the web stays out there for someone to find. It's better to take five minutes to calm down and reconsider whether you should unleash your hurt feelings on someone else.

Advice to freshman: Enjoy your time at college, but don't go telling everyone in the world about your fun. Your posts will go beyond those who care about you. If one person sees your posts that doesn't like you they may ridicule you. Or worse, it could tarnish your long term reputation when you are applying for internships, study-abroad programs, and jobs.

Real life activities that impress colleges

What you do in real life will eventually end up on social media. Therefore, we're going to give you suggestions on what to do in real life that may impress colleges.

·   Consider volunteering at one of these organizations near you:
·   Dog shelter
·   Senior citizen center or assisted living facility
·   Overseas volunteer work
·   Habitat for Humanity
·   Red Cross or other blood donation facilities
·   Hospitals
·   Fundraising for any of these (not for a political or dramatic cause)
·   or an international summer volunteer program abroad

Make sure that what you volunteer for is not political or could be in any way seen as a dramatic. Keep in mind that college admissions officers might have different political or religious views, and you don't want your volunteer work to be off-putting.

As an example: There was a nationwide surge in 2012 of activists and regular people promoting a 30-minute video titled, "Kony 2012." The goal of the video was to bring attention to Joseph Kony, a Ugandan warlord who commanded a rebel army that was trying to overthrow the Ugandan government. He was notorious for using children as soldiers, free labor, and sex slaves. The video brought attention to these facts in an attempt to have him arrested and humanitarian effort to be given. The intent was good and many people donated money and tweeted/posted a lot for the organization who started the video.

Unfortunately, when the video was shown to Ugandan people it was protested against and not welcomed. Major criticism for the "movement" was that it (and the video, in particular) oversimplified the issue. The rebel-government conflicts in Uganda spread much farther than just Joseph Kony. The video was also criticized for insinuating that the only way to solve the conflicts were for people from outside the country to send help in; while in fact, there were several initiatives already going on, led by locals to solve their problems.

The Kony 2012 organization was later found to be misusing donated funds and their founder was seen in the media as very unstable.

Whenever you find a movement that's highly political or highly emotional, be hesitant to publicly promote it until you have time to research both sides of the story. Without investigating the bigger picture, your social media post about the campaign could come back to haunt you, because you don't know where it will be in the next few years.

The original fundraising video went viral very fast. The problem was that few people actually did research behind the organization who started it, or behind the issue at large. So now that new truths have been revealed about the leadership at Kony, a college reviewing your social media could see that you ended up being a bandwagon fan for this controversial movement, and you aligned yourself with this questionable campaign.

Tactical Tip: Whenever you find a movement that's highly political or highly emotional, be hesitant to publicly promote it until you have time to research both sides of the story. Without investigating the bigger picture, your social media post about the campaign could come back to haunt you, because you don't know where it will be in the next few years.

As an alternative, pick an established organization and

volunteer for them. Consider not starting out by volunteering with a brand new campaign, because there may be things you don't know about them. Ask yourself: Is this one campaign something that could taint my online image in the next five years if something goes wrong? Also, don't assume that your college admission officer votes or agrees with your stance on the issue. You are just as likely to offend them as you are to make yourself stand out. That's a fifty-fifty chance of upsetting them if you post anything that's highly emotional or political.

Networks that can help your online image

Social networks are like TV networks: Some are designed to make you smarter and others are designed to pass time. If you watch an hour of Discovery Channel, you'll come away learning something (or at least feel as though your mind was somewhat stimulated). However, if you watch an hour of "Keeping Up With the Kardashians" you'll probably come away with very little useful info. I'm not saying that watching reality TV is terrible, I'm just saying that you're much less inclined to come away with anything tangible, for the amount of time that you invested. With that in mind, I strongly believe that some social networks are more like the Discovery channel (and can be a positive use of your kid's time).

In chapter five, I walk you through different networks and what they can do to help your online image. Consider having a profile on these networks to have a well-rounded and discoverable online presence. Just because your college says that they don't look at your social media, the likelihood that they will search for you in the next few years is going to increase rapidly. A school isn't going to invest in someone they haven't researched carefully. Searching online for applicants is becoming part of the standard protocol. You can use this to your advantage to stand out from the pack.

Gratitude is the most exquisite form of courtesy.
– Jacques Maritain

Ways a college invests in you when they consider accepting you:

- You become their personal brand (and represent them for the rest of your life)
- They can't accept another person in your place (they only accept so many students)
- Scholarships require them to spend money on your tuition (and they forfeit revenue from a paying student)

When a school offers you acceptance they are immediately making an investment because they are allowing you to represent them everywhere you go. (Especially in your home town and on your social media profiles). The college wants to maintain a positive image because this helps them to impress future students, alumni and donors to attend their university in the future. On top of that, giving you a scholarship is an even bigger investment. It all comes down to the practical nature of the situation: because a college has a limited amount of spots and resources, they need to research you before they make an offer.

> *You don't have to be great to start, but you have to start to be great.*
> – Zig Ziglar

Owning the first page of your online search results

When a college searches for your name online, what do they find? Do they see a set of results on the first page that paints a positive picture of who you are in real life? If not, what comes up?

A college should be able to quickly find a portfolio of your accomplishments, volunteer pictures, fun videos, and/or creative and productive pastimes. The first page of your Google search results is truly your place to shine online. When you are on several different established social media networks and you have your own website, you have a lot of places to post content that casts you in the best light. Use this place to showcase your talents, interests and abilities so that colleges can see you as an engaged and intelligent student who would make a great addition to their institution.

Are your search results helping you to shine online? If you're following the guidelines and formulas that we give you, you may be less inclined to block your accounts from the public since you will have nothing hindering you from sharing all of your positive experiences and putting your best foot forward.

Also, I want to encourage you to share your hobbies in a way that helps colleges see that you're well-rounded and a safe bet for their investment.

> *An investment in knowledge pays the best interest.*
> *- Benjamin Franklin*

Of course, always follow general internet safety. If you are under 13, please talk to your parents about what privacy settings they prefer. From a professional standpoint, you'll rely on privacy settings a lot less when using my techniques, making you look more open to review from colleges (and hopefully letting you stand out from the crowd).

Use the same profile photo for all of your accounts

When colleges search for you they want to quickly be assured they found the right account. They are searching for hundreds of applicants each day and when you have different selfies for each network you're going to make it difficult for them to find you. Seeing the same photo on each account makes it easier for the college to connect the dots between all of your professional, fun, relevant forms of social media. Make sure that your photo is clear, well-lit, and highlights only you (obscure group photos will not help you). Consider the previous chapter and make sure that every part of the photo is Light, Bright and Polite®. When in doubt, ask a parent or friend for their thoughts on the best photo. Sometimes you may not realize which of your photos highlights your best features in a fun and professional manner. I still run many of my accounts past friends to get their honest feedback from an outside perspective. It's always good to get a second opinion.

Worried about how much time this takes? Owning your online image is a commitment of about one hour per week. Make sure to check all networks for at least five minutes per week. Spend a few minutes on your least favorite professional networks at the beginning of every week. Make sure that you are updating your information and credentials frequently so that nothing is inaccurate or stale. If time is a concern, try HootSuite.com or BufferApp.com to help plan social media posts and then walk away knowing it doesn't need thinking about until the next planning session.

Formula for posting

The way you post will either help or hurt you, as we've talked about in previous chapters. We're going to show you a formula here that will help you put your best foot forward so that when a college sees it, it will help add value to your application in a way that can't be done on paper. This formula is optional, but it may be something that can help you online since we developed it to help politicians, college applicants, job applicants, and some of the world's best brands.

Here's a formula to impress colleges:

Tasteful group photo

+

Thanks

+

Organization name

+

Activity

+

Outcome

Take a tasteful group photo

As an example, take a group photo of your team volunteering to work with dogs, build houses for Habitat for Humanity, serving with the Red Cross in Hatai. Don't use this as a moment to make the photo about yourself when it's really about the cause. Don't include any gestures that might be funny or misunderstood. Make sure everyone's face is clear, with a genuine smile, and everyone is there for the right reason. Here are some examples in action:

How to take a group photo with your coworkers:

Here's a good example from my friend Lisa Kanazawa who works at Disneyland Parks:

"Special thanks to my team at Disneyland Parks for all that they do to make dreams come true at the most magical place on earth."

"Thank you to Shelter Hope Pet Shop for letting us share some of our tech tips with you. Keep up the great work helping these dogs find loving homes!"

How to thank your friends for baseball tickets:

Here's a sports game example from my friend Camille Marquez:

"Thanks to my friends for inviting me to join them in these great seats. Go Dodgers!"

How to take a great family photo:

Here's another example from my friend Camille Marquez on how to take an impromptu family photo:

"It's days like this that make me thankful for my family and the great weather while we hunt for Easter Eggs in the backyard."

How to volunteer at the Special Games:
Here's one last example of Camille Marquez as she volunteers at the Special Games with her friends:

"Thanks to my friends for helping to make this day a wonderful experience for our friend Steve who participated in the Special Games. A great day was had by all."

How to thank families that visited an educational field trip:
Here's an example of me volunteering at the local airport to show kids the joy of aviation:

"Thank you to the volunteers that helped us give 100+ kids the chance to sit in a real airplane today at Santa Monica Airport."

How to thank a foundation and a mayor:

"Thank you to the 'Walk With Sally Foundation' for inviting me to participate in tonight's charity event. It was great bumping into my old friend Michael DiVirgilio, the next Mayor of Hermosa Beach."

How to thank an event sponsor:

"Thank you to UCLA Anderson MBA School of Management for inviting me to share my message on a TED Talk panel discussion."

How to be positive after a power outage:

Here's an example of a past student named Elise Arney that currently attends University of Kansas. When the power went out that day at her home, she could have complained, but took this approach instead. If a college admission officer sees this picture, they will probably say, "If this is how she complains, then we need her positive attitude setting a good example for other students. Let's get her here to interview!"

"So thankful to have such a great family! Had a great day even with our power outage!"

How to take a photo with a college mascot:

Here's a photo of Elise visiting KU after she was accepted,

taking a photo next to the mascot in a way that makes the college proud of their decision to accept her.

"Had so much fun on my college visit to KU today! So ready for next year!"

How to reach out to colleges in a way that's charming and shows a sense of humor:

Here's an example of a high school student named Jonathan Yee who knew colleges would look at his social media, so he took a picture of a handwritten note and posted it on Twitter:

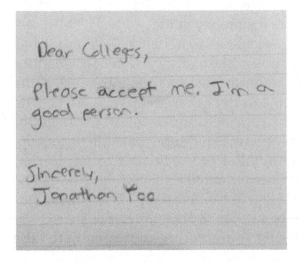

"Finished my college apps"

How to thank a sponsor for letting you perform:

I could have put under the image: "I spoke to 50 kids this weekend at Microsoft stores!" That would make it all about ME, and less about the bigger picture. It doesn't give credit to the organization that made my speech possible and it doesn't show that I have gratitude for that incredible opportunity.

Improved message: "Thank you to the Microsoft for allowing me to host a Social Media Safety tour in four of their stores in Southern California this week. With their help we positively impacted over 100 kids." This message takes me out of the spotlight and focuses on the positive outcome of what I was able to participate in.

The social media frequency guide

Consider posting once a week on all networks (even the ones that we listed that you don't like visiting). You don't want to flood everything onto your accounts at once, because some great stuff can get buried under other great stuff. To get the most coverage of all of your accomplishments, spread out when you upload posts. Again, HootSuite.com and BufferApp. com can help. Just remember to check your content every week and update or replace outdated information. Tips can be found here on what tools you can use to space out messages and deploy information: SafeSmartSocial.com/book

Own your image by volunteering your camera to take group photos

When I ran for politics I would always want to post the best photo of the group while also managing my reputation. Since I always had a camera or a cell phone with me, before a group photo, I'd be the one to volunteer, "Use my phone." This let me always be in on the fun, but also let me control what kinds of pictures were posted (since they all lived on my phone/camera). That way, no crazy or inappropriate pictures started to circulate online or otherwise. I was able to select the best photo to post. I picked ones that highlighted me and made my friends look great. I became my own brand manager and helped my friends stand out online. This is one of those tactical tips that helped me to impress voters during my political race (and the reason I have clean Google image results).

Wait until after the event to post your photos

If you attend a lot of fun events, you may have a lot of

photos to post. Consider waiting until the next day to post any of your event photos. This gives you time to think of a great description, and you get to pick the best photo that you took. You could even use Photoshop to clear up the photo, or upload the organization's logo into the picture (like I did with Microsoft). This also helps you to be less distracted while you're at the event so that you don't miss possibly another great opportunity to take an additional photo. Lastly, you'll have a chance the next day to be a good friend on social media and select the photo where all of your friends also shine online. This helps you to stand out since you're managing your own brand (and that of your friends) online.

Social Media Gardening with your BFF

Who is your best friend or your most trusted friend? Ask them to look at all of your social media accounts and find three things you posted that they think you should remove. The story behind the picture could be completely innocent, but to outsiders it may look unbecoming. Tell your BFF or your close friend that whatever they say, your feelings won't be hurt. Their honesty will help you have the best online image. This helped me keep my image clean during politics when a friend gave me some honest feedback that helped me shine online during my campaign. It's better for this to come from your BFF than to be clueless or unaware that your posts are keeping you from impressing colleges.

Parent Challenge

Sometimes parents think their kids are "perfect," but they are really blind to their children's faults on social media. As a parent, you could partner with other parents you know, who have similar goals for their children, and you can swap the responsibilities of keeping their children Light, Bright, and Polite® online. One parent can mentor the other parent's kids to guide their online image. The outside advice from another trusted parent usually will do more good than harm, and could provide new perspective that helps you (or your kids) shine online.

This is something that parents can do without the help of an expert. It's just you working with another family to make sure that both of your kids are keeping it professional.

Map out your future - but do it in pencil. The road ahead is as long as you make it. Make it worth the trip
-Jon Bon Jovi

Parents know when they see something cringe-worthy, even when kids don't think of it like that. This can take you out of the "my kid is perfect" bubble.

Alternately, you could befriend an HR manager or college professor and have them talk with your kids. This would help to bring real world examples directly to your kid's mind so they are getting valid feedback from someone that researches candidates and applicants every day.

What if you're applying to college next month? How do you ramp this up? Over the next 10 days begin to post one positive photo per day on LinkedIn, Facebook, Instagram and Twitter to start your portfolio. The goal is to get 10 photos online in less than two weeks. That's the minimum amount of pictures you need to look present and get discovered online. Even if you aren't on Facebook, consider putting photos there since colleges will easily find that account.

Designate someone you trust as your personal "brand manager" who can check on your posts each week. This person can be your BFF, your favorite teacher or one of your parents. Their goal is to let you know if you posted something inappropriate that week and why you should remove it. It helps to have this objective second person who can review what you're posting and be honest with you about what message it sends to those around you. Not enough people have this and if you enlist someone to help, they become your brand manager.

Visit SafeSmartSocial.com/book to register this book for free and we will send you videos and key takeaways to help your students use social media to impress colleges and employers.

Key takeaways from this chapter:

- People are biased toward remembering negative things. Always think twice before posting something.
- Take a break before posting a frustrated comment.
- Write an email to someone sharing with them all of your angry or hurt thoughts. Don't address the "TO" field. Walk away for at least five minutes. If you're still upset, consider sending it to a safe and trustworthy friend.
- When having upsetting conversations, start with the heart. Appreciate the person, share your feelings, give them an "out" and ask for their opinion on the situation. Try to empathize with them and they will more likely empathize with you. Good relationships fuel good behavior and good reputations.

  All our dreams can come true if we have the courage to pursue them.
  – Walt Disney

- Parents set the example for their kids in how to behave online.
- Good posts for social media show volunteer work and fundraising.
- Be sure to research organizations and causes you support. Ensure they have stood the test of time, unlike Kony 2012.
- Colleges are looking for people who represent their brand.
- Own the first page of your Google search results for your name or name + location.
- Visible posts should include: accomplishments, volunteer photos, creative and productive pastimes, and positive and fun things.
- Use the same profile photo on all of your accounts.
- Set aside an hour a week to reevaluate, update, and post on social media. Consider trying HootSuite.com or BufferApp.com to help manage posts.

- When taking a photo at an organization or event, be sure to thank them, to mention their name, to say what you did and what the outcome was.
- Do not make volunteering or fundraising opportunities about you. It's about the cause.
- Offer your camera for group photos so that you own the image and control how your image is shared. You'll be able to choose the best photo. Just be sure to follow through with posting and emailing it to people as you said you would.
- Ask a best friend for feedback on what photos of yours they think you should remove.
- Parents, with the problem of not having enough distance to see that their kid may not be seen in the best of light by someone else, can try asking friends or siblings to help give feedback on their kid's online image.

CHAPTER FOUR
Social media posts and strategies that impress future employers

---

If you think in terms of a year, plant a seed; if you think in terms of ten years, plant trees; if in terms of 100 years, teach the people. –Confucius

---

I've hired quite a few employees over the past five years and I am going to give some tips that college students can use to stand out from the crowd on social media. I've also been in a position early in my career to have attended about 100 interviews as I was trying to jumpstart my future and find out where I wanted to work. These interviews helped me to put my best foot forward in person and online.

We're also going to give college students some tips on how to get ahead of the crowd by using social media and some old school techniques with new digital tools.

Lisa Cochrane, Senior Vice President of Marketing at Allstate Insurance Corp., gives college students looking for their first professional job the four following pieces of advice:

Be authentic and professional

First, be authentic. Trying to impress versus impressing are two different things. Let your real self shine through, but think about and curate what the public can see when they search you. Not everything about your authentic self is for public viewing. For example, you could make your Facebook private but strategically choose a few posts and photos to set as "public". Make two or three of your best profile pictures public (great shot of you, you in an interesting place, doing something in the community, with your family, etc.) and any posts about career interests, school, volunteering, your most recent work (if you're an artist, writer, etc.), press clips, etc. If someone is searching to find information about you online, this is a good way not to seem totally closed-off and still control exactly what you want people to know about you.

> Having another organization speak for your performance is more valuable than self-promotion.

Always consider an outsider's perspective before you share socially or voice an opinion. Others don't know you as well as your personal network and may judge you out of context.

Tactical Tip: If you're active in nonprofit and/or professional organizations (whether in school or outside), ask to be given a bio on their website or spotlighted in their blog as a core volunteer or member. Having another organization speak for your performance is more valuable than self-promotion.

Are you a good writer?

I always look for good communication skills. Although the world has changed and texting and email allow for a more informal and conversational writing style, there's still no replacement for good, old-fashioned English used well. Use correct spelling, grammar and punctuation. While "OMG" and "ROFL" work in your personal network, they don't transfer well into the professional world.

Tactical Tip: Choose your words wisely -- less is sometimes more.

Show you've thought about your future

Consider using separate social media handles for publishing personal and professional content. Having a public Twitter and LinkedIn where you share industry-relevant content and ideas (don't go overboard, choose wisely) will demonstrate your passion and knowledge in your field(s).

If you deliver a notable speech or performance that somebody captures on video (think about this in advance and make sure you have a designated videographer), upload it to YouTube and make it searchable with your name.

> You don't have to create your own blog, but do consider contributing to forums and blogs related to your carer interests and/or passions.

Tactical Tip: You don't have to create your own blog, but do consider contributing to forums and blogs related to your career interests and/or passions. When doing this, use your full name as your username.

Demonstrate you know how to work, unafraid to get your hands dirty

I always look for an indicator that a prospective candidate likes to work. Did you wait tables or work in retail? That's a sign of humility and that you know how to work with the public —you probably appreciate a good customer experience. Did you work while in school? Then you must be good at time management and respect the value of a dollar. All jobs teach you something—even the worst jobs.

Here are some activities that employers like to discover on social media:

· Volunteering to help others (non political activities) like working at a dog shelter, assisted living home, hospital, etc.

· Being involved in subjects you are passionate about that help others or help you grow as a person. That could include running for a cause, traveling, building cars, sailing, cooking, playing an instrument or other hobbies

that make you more well-rounded.
- Internships and work related projects that relate to the position you are applying for.

Here are some activities that employers DO NOT want to see on social media:
- Photos of you holding a red cup at a party
- Selfies of you acting silly or narcissistic
- Inside jokes that are crude in nature
- Photos of you at a famous landmark being disrespectful
- Sharing photos of your friends being irresponsible
- Illegal actions (or skirting around the rules) and thinking it's funny to share
- Complaining about a past job, boss, professor or work related situation
- Bragging online about actions that could negatively impact your future (or others)
- Not being appreciative of good people, situations, and opportunities
- Bragging about getting away with lying to a former employer or cheating them out of work time

Never forget to thank your employer and those who helped you accomplish your goals

When I become a political candidate I needed to surround myself with trustworthy people who also looked out for my image. I was fortunate that one of my closest friends accepted my request to volunteer as my campaign manager in 2009 when I was running for city council in Hermosa Beach. Her name is Jessica McIntyre and she currently works in HR at Nestlé.

> *Never make negative comments or spread rumors about anyone. It depreciates their reputation and yours.*
> *- Brian Koslow*

I trusted Jessica with my image on the campaign trail

and she always made great decisions. When impressing employers, Jessica recommends:

"It's always a good idea when posting something on social media to compliment those that you work for. Whenever you can sincerely thank your employer/team for giving you the chance to work on a project, you're usually going to impress them when (not if) they find it on social media."

Use social media to your advantage

Social media is quickly becoming the preferred method of connecting with those around us. You can use this to your advantage by learning as much about online courtesy and protocol as you can.

Ryan Holmes, CEO of Hootsuite, the largest social media platform in the world, says:

Social media is no longer just for sharing cute pet photos with your friends. In the right hands, it's a powerful tool—your social media profiles can mean the difference in finding and keeping a job. Use social networks like LinkedIn to create a professional and attractive brand online and woo prospective employers. The great thing about social media is that you can control what others see and know about you. So make sure you use networks to your advantage by building a professional personal brand that is, well, professional.

> *Employees are a company's greatest asset - they're your competitive advantage. You want to attract and retain the best; provide them with encouragement, stimulus, and make them feel that they are an integral part of the company's mission.*
> – Anne M. Mulcahy

Do employers like entrepreneurial projects?

Displaying how entrepreneurial you are on your social media accounts can be very positive. However, make sure you highlight how that action or project helps others and has a positive outcome that is worth sharing. If you have an entrepreneurial spirit, it is better to highlight how your entrepreneurial project did a good deed in the community, so that you don't seem self-focused to a possible employer that is worried about you trying to start your own business on their dime.

Wait, are you saying it's bad to show off your entrepreneurial side?

No, but the job of your boss or hiring manager is to find someone who can fit well into their company and their culture. To paint that picture, you need to appear helpful and hard working. You want to be a go-getter that can achieve all around positive outcomes. Sometimes candidates (myself included) will show off how they can lead on social media but they don't actually show any sign of staying focused or working hard at the details.

Turn your projects into a positive story

For example, let's say you want to start a new club on campus that will bring all kinds of people together that are very passionate about website design. It's called the "Website Design Club." The club builds websites for organizations that can't afford the service. The club's websites become better and better with each site they create, and they can promote that they have trained small businesses how to create their own websites and they've built websites for certain foundations free of charge.

> *Always do your best. What you plant now, you will harvest later.*
> –Og Mandino

Now you and other members can publish a list of the foundations that they've worked with. The project will turn out to help thousands of people, and because the websites you built were organized and easy to use, they have raised thousands of dollars towards their causes. Employers will love to see this and want to hire people from this "website design club" because of the positive outcome of this activity. This is one of many real life examples of an entrepreneurial mission that can be highlighted as a project that helped others and will eventually impress employers.

Be a leader with what you already know

Don't go pick up new skills just to use them to brag online. Take what you already have and grow there. Don't try and start a new, extensive hobby just to show off. Instead, work on improving what you can already do and have it help others. Be prepared to explain what your hobby means to you, how it has influenced your life, work ethic, motivation, etc., and how you were a leader in that situation.

Find your one thing and do that one thing better than anyone else.
– Jason Goldberg

As an example, I can't play any musical instruments. It would take me many years to get comfortable playing the piano or guitar well enough to be able to use those skills to help others. However, I realized early on that I'm really good with power tools and very handy at fixing household appliances and cars. Instead of playing the guitar, my instrument is a power drill and a hammer. I can help others by using these tools and share the positive outcome on social media. With very little extra time, I can volunteer by repairing items and use that experience as a positive story to share a group photo online. In some cases I have used this technique to create YouTube videos to teach others how they can learn my skills to repair their vehicles or appliances.

Choose your words wisely — less is sometimes more.

Use YouTube to share your skills

One day I noticed a headlamp was defective on my Jeep Grand Cherokee. I took it to the dealership and they wanted about $350 to replace both headlights with parts and labor. At the time, my car was about 13 years old and I did a little research to find that many people had the same problem.

When I went to Amazon.com I found that I could buy a new pair of headlamps for $80. I then planned out how I was going to fix my Jeep and show others how to save $270 by doing it themselves. As I was replacing the headlamps, I used my iPhone to record small segments of the repair and edited them into a 4 minute how-to video. The video now has over 7,000 views. Although the video isn't inline with my profession, if a client discovered it online they would be impressed that I'm helping others with my skills.

What top employers look for in candidates

My friend Julie Mossler is the Head of Global Communications and Creative Launch Strategy at Waze, an innovative mapping application acquired by Google. She offers those seeking employment the following advice:

> Always weed those old posts! "Younger you" was cool and knew everything, or so you thought at the time. Now, the "new you" knows even more. What seemed like a good thing to share two years ago may not jive with who you are as a person or job candidate anymore. There is no harm in deleting stale content when it doesn't fairly represent who you are today, especially when it can help you shine online to a potential employer.

Consistency is key. If you're respectful and professional tweets are peppered with arguments with friends or a significant other, I will assume your judgment is poor. No one wants to read your drama online! It makes me consider, Will you do that when you represent our brand, too? There's a level of your personal life the internet doesn't need to know about – learn that comfort zone, and stay within the box.

Julie goes on to give this insight:

> When I'm reviewing candidates for a job opening, I am more impressed by someone who is smart enough

to pick one social channel and do it well than someone who has a thin, scattered online presence. I don't care if you don't have all of Facebook, Twitter, LinkedIn and Google Plus mastered. I do care if you started a profile in one place and it hasn't been updated in a year or your posts demonstrate that you don't understand the channel. Not staying up-to-date on something makes you look unprofessional, especially compared to the other candidates that I'm reviewing. It's not about being a social media expert, it's about how much effort you put in. If you did or didn't take the time to create a profile and do it well (update content, keep the layout clean and professional, etc.), that either demonstrates thoroughness or laziness.

Focus on what you do best and stay involved! If you have a Facebook or Twitter account that you haven't posted relevant and professional content to in quite some time, you don't appear present. Remember to keep posting Light, Bright, and Polite.®

Tactical Tip: Focus on what you do best and stay involved! If you have a Facebook or Twitter account that you haven't posted relevant and professional content to in quite some time, you don't appear present. Remember to keep posting Light, Bright, and Polite® material as well as deleting old or irrelevant content.

Formula for posting

This formula is going to be very similar to the one used in the previous chapter to impress colleges. A lot of the fundamentals are the same, except that in high school you're taking photos of everything from family outings to your sporting events. In college, you are taking pictures of group projects, internships and fun activities.

Group photo steps for success
At the end of every group project, take a picture with the entire group. If you're in an internship, ask if you can take an approved group photo with your peers and/or a customer.

Here's a formula for posting to your social media accounts:

Take a tasteful group photo
(Of you in a leadership position or on a group project)
+
Sincere thanks for the opportunity to participate
+
Organization name
+
Activity/purpose of the event you participated in
+
Outcome of your work

Remember to be humble and genuine in all of your posts.

Here are some examples of this formula:

How to thank an organization for a volunteer opportunity:

"Thank you to the Boys and Girls Club of Greater Washington DC for inviting me to share with their kids how to be safe on social media!"

How to thank a client after a project:

"Thank you to the Salvation Army for inviting me to share my social media tactics with their team this month."

How to announce a great opportunity:

"Thank you to Vistage for inviting me to train their 50 CEOs today on marketing best practices."

How to share a networking opportunity:

"Thanks to Commercial Real Estate Women (CREW) for inviting me to visit them in Sacramento to share my LinkedIn Boot Camp tips."

How to announce a volunteer opportunity:

"Thank you to USC Kappa Alpha Theta Sorority for inviting me to teach "LinkedIn Bootcamp to Impress Employers.""

How to thank a large group of volunteers:

"Thank you to the 12+ volunteers that helped us inspire 250+ kids to learn more about STEM education at Santa Monica Airport."

Possible message to use below an internship photo:

"Thank you to my company (company name) for the great opportunity to intern with them. If you haven't visited their site it is xyz.com and they make organic dog food that helps dogs with joint problems. I got to work on a project with seven other interns over the last month and we were able to study and implement new nutritious supplements that can be added to their line of dog treats. I am so thankful for this opportunity!"

This is a little different from the previous chapter's formula because your photos have a different substance. Make sure you are using a productive photo and that you include the group name and a sincere thank you. Again, be specific about what you did and what the outcome was.

Tactical Tip: Your current and future employers are more inclined to approve of you posting about their company when you give a sincere THANK YOU to them for the chance to work there (and helping them to promote a specific project or client). Use caution, though, because once you post something about an employer, you are always and irrevocably tied to that company. Anything else that you post, even if it is personal and has nothing to do with a work situation, will reflect on your employer and their company. For that reason, make sure that you are Light, Bright, and Polite® in everything you do online so that there is not a chance of you embarrassing your employer and getting yourself into a lot of trouble with them.

> Anything you post, even if it is personal and has nothing to do with a work situation, will reflect on your employer and their company. So, make sure that you are Light, Bright, and Polite® in everything you do online so that there is no chance to embarrass your employer and getting yourself into trouble.

Along the same idea, you can take a tasteful group photo at the beginning of a business networking event or social hour. Make sure everyone puts down (or hides) their drinks, or any red cups, and takes a classy group photo to highlight how social the event is. Have everyone squeeze together with genuine smiles and look directly at the camera.

Tactical Tip: Have your photographer snap 5-6 photos of your group shot. That ensures you'll get at least one photo with everyone looking their best.

FAQs

Will my kid look like everyone else if they follow your advice?

Chances are, probably not. People are so different, that 90% of the people who read this book will put my formula into effect in different ways. Unfortunately, some kids won't use these techniques at all. If kids do use these techniques to stand out, they are likely going to use the formula in a way that highlights their unique take on a project. I feel very confident telling you that you will be okay and not look like everyone else when using these techniques. The chances of the employer seeing your kid doing something exactly the same as another kid is very rare. Keep in mind that we aren't giving you something to copy and paste into your kid's social media accounts. Instead, we are showing you a customizable formula for posting that shows that helps your child stand out as a well-rounded individual online.

It takes 20 years to build a reputation and five minutes to ruin it. If you think about that, you'll do things differently.
– Warren Buffett

Will my kid get in trouble for sharing company secrets?

Yes! They will get in trouble. So please in all that you do, be careful not to share anything confidential. Ask permission before you take a picture. Here's a great way to ask your employer, "Would you mind if we take a picture of this project or of our group?" nine times out of 10, they are going to say "Sure, no problem," especially if you clarify what the picture is for and where it's going to be shared to. When in doubt, don't share unless you have permission. Never share any company secrets. Instead, only allude to what is already public information and highlight the positive side of the story. Really, your post should be more about the group photo than about bragging with details.

How do I get people to want to take photos with me for this?

All you need to do is ask them. Most of the time, people would be happy to. Consider using the following phrase, "Do you mind taking a group photo with me that we could share on our blog to highlight this project?" Or, "Employer, may I take a group photo that we can share on our company Facebook page? I will take the initiative to make it look nice and do something nice for the company." Or, "Can we take a group photo that highlights the client?" or "Employer, can we take a picture with the client to say thanks to them for working with us?" The employer will typically say yes.

Then, run down the hallway to find someone else to snap the photo from the other side of the room (selfies aren't great for group photos). Try to position yourself somewhere in the middle of the pic and (if you feel comfortable) put your arms around those around you to seem like a happy crowd. You can be on the edges, but everyone loves a leader in the middle of the photo; it's just a nice little touch when you're the one sharing it. You get the opportunity to talk less about the photo when you're in the middle of the photo.

A reputation once broken may possibly be repaired, but the world will always keep their eyes on the spot where the crack was.
– Joseph Hall

Another way to ask for a photo could be: "Employer, I'm doing a group project for class about this internship. Do you mind if I take a group picture of this project I'm working on with you and then present it to my class when I'm done with this internship?"

They'll think it's great that you're sharing their information in a positive way. Assure them that you won't share any confidential information. Just about every employer will say yes to that because it's effortless, positive advertising for their group. Group photos can be a part of almost every one of your projects and internships. Then you can use that photo on your own social media (as long as it doesn't breach confidentiality) and use the formula above to craft an outstanding post.

Visit SafeSmartSocial.com/book to register this book for free and we will send you videos and key takeaways to help your students use social media to impress colleges and employers.

Key takeaways for this chapter:

- Be authentic and professional.
- Trying to impress versus impressing are two different things.
- Having another organization speak for your performance is more valuable than self-promotion.
- Choose your words wisely -- less is sometimes more.
- You don't have to create your own blog, but do try to contribute to forums and blogs related to your career interests and/or passions.
- Be a leader with what you already know.
- Always weed those old posts! There is no harm in deleting stale content when it doesn't fairly represent who you are today, especially when it can help you shine online to a potential employer.
- Consistency is key.
- Your current (and future) employers are more inclined to like you posting about their company when you give a sincere THANK YOU to them for the chance work there (and helping them to promote a specific project or client).

CHAPTER FIVE

Social networking sites that help you shine online

Children have never been very good at listening to their elders, but they have never failed to imitate them. –James A. Baldwin

I get a lot of questions from parents. "How do I fix bad posts that show up under my name on Google?" they ask. The best answer I can give is to create great content to push the bad stuff down, so you can own the first page of your Google results. You will need to get on several social media networks that will help you push bad posts down in Google search ranking, allowing the good stuff to float to the top.

Here's a list of my favorite networks that I suggest everyone use:

LinkedIn steps for success

It's a very good idea to spend a lot of time filling out all of your LinkedIn profile items with clear information that describes your work history and past projects. This is a professional form of social media. This site is the "new" way to get discovered online because it shows up on the first page of online search results when people are looking for you.

LinkedIn is the future of resumes. Gone are the days when employers trusted your PDF or Microsoft word resume without looking us up online. Nowadays they take our resume and compare it to LinkedIn to match a face to a name.

Have your kid use the same first and last name used at school and on their college admission form. Don't use a middle name unless used on the admission form.

For middle schoolers (14 year olds): It's a great chance to put up school projects and write out what they learned on each project.

For junior high schoolers (14 – 15 years old): It's a great chance to put up organizations they've joined, sports or honor clubs they're a part of, volunteer work they've done, and school projects from which they've learned.

For senior high schoolers (15 – 18 years old): It's a great chance to display all of the above, as well as trips they've been on, extra-curricular classes they've taken, their resume, work and internship experience and endorsements / recommendations.

It's good to have a thick, relevant history on LinkedIn that colleges can discover and point to as a professional home base online.

For college students (18 – 22 years old): Keep in mind that since the printed version of their resume doesn't have a picture on it, and hiring managers probably met you at an on-campus recruiting event with hundreds of other applicants, they need a clear, professional photo of themselves so they can be quickly identified.

Under each description for projects and work experience in LinkedIn, here's my technique that will help anyone stand out from the crowd:

The first line of your job description should include a one sentence description of what the organization or business does in its industry. This will help outsiders to quickly give context to your role in the company. For example, I wrote under Disney Studios: "Disney is the largest media and entertainment conglomerate in the world with revenues of $36.1 billion."

The second section of your description should include

what your role was at the company or organization. It can be bulleted or paragraph style and can be thankful in nature. For example, I wrote:

"Disney/Buena Vista Home Entertainment was a wonderful experience for me. I worked closely with seven departments and managed all areas of DVD projects from start to finish. My boss would set the stage for production, and I would assist in all meetings to track creative, operations, financials, promotions and media. I negotiated with outside vendors and had a blast winning over people in other divisions. Disney was a wonderful place to start my career and I often refer back to this job in my public speaking."

Below your job description you have the opportunity to insert bullets or a special quote from the employer they may have written to you in a letter of recommendation. One of the best forms of sales is having someone else say nice things about you. As an example, here's what I put in my third section:

Here's an excerpt from my former boss at Disney:

Josh is eager, persistent, positive and, well, people just like him. Even now, when Josh drops by for a visit employees of every level pop out of their offices to say hello. Josh's people skills are awe inspiring. And best of all, like Superman he uses his power for good, not evil. He has renegotiated deadlines, coaxed extra effort out of vendors, wheedled talent into extraordinary PR – and always, the people who work with Josh feel lucky, happy and relaxed. That's the magical part. Josh's attitude is relentlessly sunny. Throw him a moody executive, harsh feedback, an insurmountable 'No' and Josh rebounds effortlessly. His refusal to respond personally to professional setbacks helps to keep the entire team focused on the business objectives during tense and potentially contentious negotiations.

-Lisa Clements, Director of Marketing at Walt Disney Studios

Learn more of my LinkedIn tips by watching a video at SafeSmartSocial.com/book to get an exclusive set of tips you can use to setup your digital resume.

Google Plus steps for success

Google Plus is owned by Google and its results are given an unfair advantage over other social media accounts to be displayed on the first page of your search results.

When someone searches for you online, you want to own and control the first page of the search results they see, and since Google Plus is owned by Google, it's a great place to start.

If you have a Gmail address, you can quickly activate your Google Plus account with just a few clicks.

Although HR managers and college admissions use this network less than LinkedIn, this network will allow you to get discovered in Google's image results and search results much quicker, since it has an unfair advantage in Google's algorithm.

You're probably thinking that you don't have time to post on yet another account. Don't worry, all you need to do is post to your Google Plus page once a week with a clean image and message. Most of the time this can be done from your phone and be a repeat of your best Instagram posts.

It's wise to use a similar profile photo and bio as LinkedIn, Twitter, Facebook and any other networks you are on so you can easily be discovered online by those that search for you.

In addition, your Google Plus profile should display links to all of your other networks so Google can link them to your "digital identity" and use that info to serve up the most relevant results for those searching for you. This will help you to "combat" other people being displayed in your search results.

Your Google Plus account should be tied to your Gmail address so you can get updates in your inbox in case you have little time to check this network.

Google Plus Tactical Tip: Talk in the third person.

Since very few people use Google Plus, this is a great place to use photo captions in a way that helps change your Google results, without being socially awkward. Google loves search results in the third person because it appears that someone else is doing the writing. And if someone else is writing it, Google thinks it's probably more credible than if you're writing it yourself. To do so, consider including your full name in captions that describe photos. This will help to adjust your Google Image results.

> *A word of encouragement from a teacher to a child can change a life. A word of encouragement from a leader can inspire a person to reach their potential.*
> – John C. Maxwell

Example: "Thank you to the Orange County Animal Shelter for letting Josh Ochs and his friends volunteer to help seven dogs find homes this weekend."

On Instagram it would feel very awkward to talk about yourself in a third person while your friends are following you, however, on Google Plus this technique works just fine.

Your personal website steps for success — Example: JoshOchs.com

When people search my name online as "Josh Ochs," it's my goal to have Google and Bing quickly be able to recognize my personal website as the authority with those keywords. This is why I purchased JoshOchs.com and have slowly been adding content to it over the last several years.

Buying your own website and domain name is a great way for you to quickly own something online that can eventually help you control the first page of your search results. This becomes a part of your identity on the web. Here you can start your own portfolio of accomplishments and update it on a regular basis. Whether it's athletics, social work, volunteering, etc. you can post photos and videos to your own website so that search engines will put you above other random results.

To see how we setup our sites, visit SafeSmartSocial.com/book and register this book to watch a free set of videos on WordPress.

My real first name is Joshua but people call me Josh. Therefore, I bought the domain with the exact spelling that people use to search for me online: JoshOchs.com. If having both names is important to you, you could possibly buy the formal spelling of your name and have it forwarded to the more common spelling.

Although you want to use the domain that includes the spelling of your name that people will search for, it's also smart to buy the misspelling of your name (in my case I have a last name that is misspelled often). As an example: I own JoshOaks.com and JoshOchs.com. I direct the traffic from the misspelled domain to the correctly spelled domain. It's an investment to have people discover me and not get lost. If you visit JoshOaks.com you will be instantly forwarded to JoshOchs.com.

Once you have your website built, you can add projects, resumes, and volunteer work at least once per month. The more often you share relevant helpful content, the more likely that search engines will see that your website is dynamic and helpful for people to display on the first page of their Google results.

Have other people look over your website and provide you with tips so you can make the messaging and pictures tell the best story about your accomplishments. The site doesn't have to be very fancy; the story of your accomplishments and portfolio are the most important parts.

Facebook steps for success

Have a Facebook profile even if you think it is outdated. Managers are still using Facebook to look for you. Employers do have time to look for you online, and you want to use it to get ahead of the pack.

This is a great place for you to post photos and descriptions of jobs and volunteer work you've done.

Don't be lazy online, just because you don't think people will find it. Consider this: if it's online, people will find it. If it's online, you had better be proud of it because when it does get discovered, it's either going to be the up button on the elevator of your career or it's going to be the down button. Every post will either take you up or down.

Use your real name as someone would spell it in an interview.

If your security settings are set to friends only, or friends of friends only, consider making a select few of your best pictures public so that your profile is the first to be discovered instead of someone else's by mistake.

While colleges check LinkedIn for your professional presence, they are increasingly checking Facebook for your personal presence. This is just as important to them since you'll be on their campus in both personal and professional environments.

Keep it clean by not letting people automatically tag you in photos without it requiring your approval. Also don't let people automatically check you in online at venues since it may not be somewhere that makes you shine online. Even if you're at a simple coffee shop, your friend may check you in and on your profile it may read: "I'm at Big Daddy's Beans!" which might not seem appropriate to an outsider who could easily misunderstand the venue's name.

It makes sense to keep your Facebook account set to "friends online" as a default setting. But if you're trying to impress colleges, you might consider cleaning up any inappropriate photos or posts on your Facebook so that you can make it public and have many of your volunteer activities and accomplishments displayed on your profile. Or, you can set certain posts to show as public.

Even if your Facebook is hidden, make sure you are making Light, Bright, and Polite® posts. Anything can be found on the internet (and many of your best friends might accidentally comment/share something that gets your photos discovered).

If you are 13–15 years old, it's probably smart to keep your profile private.

However, if you are 16–19 years old (and colleges/ employers are starting to search for you) it may be time to begin cleaning up their profile and making it public to get discovered doing good things online.

Twitter steps for success

Consider creating a clear and concise bio that puts your best foot forward online (without giving away too much personal information). If you're over 15, talk with your parents about being clear with your bio. Don't quote your favorite movie or song. Instead, consider making the bio about yourself, casting yourself in the brightest light. Perhaps it could sound like this: "I love softball and I'm honored to be the starting pitcher of my high school's team."

Another good example: "I'm a senior at Orange County High School and I love football, volunteering, and traveling."

Make sure you use your real name and that it is spelled in a similar manner to how you expect a college to search for you online. This will help your Twitter handle reach the first page of your search results.

Let me use myself as an example: My profile name is "Josh Ochs" (the way a college would search for me) and my username is @JoshOchs (making it easier for search engines to see me as the real Josh Ochs and making it easy for colleges to make the connection). This ensures that my Twitter handle will come up on the first page during a search for "Josh Ochs" on Google or Bing.

Here's what not to do on Twitter:

For example, a bad username for Christina Smith is: @HotBody37 and her bio reads: "I missed you ever since I found out that I would never see you again." The username Christina selected tells colleges she doesn't want to be taken seriously online. Also, her bio is indirect and slightly dramatic. It doesn't help a college decide if she's the real Christina Smith they are looking for. Since college admission officers have so little time to research while your application is on their desk, you need to ensure that you're easy to find across all networks.

> *Technology is just a tool. In terms of getting the kids working together and motivating them, the teacher is the most important.*
> – Bill Gates

What should you share on Twitter?

Twitter is a great place to share some of your most positive Instagram photos that create a portfolio of your accomplishments. Also, it's a great place to share positive quotes that are inspirational to others. Be careful not to share overly dramatic quotes.

If you are 13–15 years old, it's probably smart to keep your profile private. However, if you are 16–19 years old (and colleges/employers are starting to search for you) it may be time to begin cleaning up your profile and making it public to get discovered online. If you keep your Twitter profile private after age 19, employers and colleges might wonder what you're trying to hide, since Twitter is mostly designed to be a public bulletin board.

How can teachers responsibly interact with students using social media?

It's going to be more and more difficult to engage with students online. Here's an idea from Facebook's social media safety guide that might work for you:

Maintaining a page or group is a great way to establish a presence as a teacher without blurring the line between your personal and professional lives. You can interact with parents, students and colleagues via your page or group, called something like 'Ms. Smith's 9th Grade Science Class.'

Instagram steps for success

As with Twitter, create a distinct, clear bio on Instagram with a username that is easy for search engines to match to your real name (Look at my profile @JoshOchs or Instagram. com/JoshOchs as an example on Instagram). Be very clear about who you are and use the same profile picture that you did for every other site. This will help to connect the dots between all your profiles.

Since Instagram is so widely used, it's easy for several profiles to come up under your name. Having a uniform picture and clear bio will identify you and ward off any confusion of other accounts seeming as yours.

Instagram can be part of a well balanced reputation across several networks. As always, make sure everything you post on Instagram is Light, Bright and Polite®.

If you're trying to impress colleges, you might consider cleaning up any inappropriate photos on your Instagram so you can keep it public and have many of your volunteer activities discovered on your profile. Have your BFF/bestie look through your profile and tell you what images you should delete before making your Instagram public.

The art of teaching is the art of assisting discovery.
– Mark Van Doren

Also note, if you share most of your private Instagram photos on Twitter (and your Twitter isn't private) then you're really making your Instagram account public with each post. It's very easy for someone to visit your Twitter account and search through your Instagram photos to circumvent the privacy settings. Your reputation could possibly spill over into these other networks.

If you're 13-15 years old, it's probably smart to keep your profile private. However, if you're 16-19 years old (and colleges/employers are starting to search for you) it may be time to begin cleaning up your profile and making it public to get discovered online. Talk to your parents before you do this, so you are all on the same page.

YouTube steps for success

Since YouTube is owned by Google, it is also given unfair advantage in search results. Google knows that people love video and that's why videos will usually appear on the first page of search results in a query.

It's a good idea to tie your YouTube account to your Google Plus name so you can use one login to control them all.

Provide a link in your YouTube profile that links to your Google Plus profile so Google can see that you're starting to weave your online web.

If you have projects or videos of you volunteering, you might consider asking your friend or parent if the content would be a good fit for a college to discover online. If so, then consider putting them on your YouTube account as a public video so you can build out this very important profile. Every Mac and PC comes with some free video editing software that will let you lightly edit the clips and add an introduction title to explain the video. This ensures that your videos tell the right story on YouTube.

Don't flood your YouTube account with videos to entertain your friends. Instead, keep it Light, Bright and Polite® in each video and make sure to add value for those who might watch the video. As an example: If you Google "Josh Ochs Jeep" you will find one of my most popular YouTube videos where I share with people how to repair their headlights in their Jeep Grand Cherokee. It has received thousands of views and lots of comments. This video is something I'm OK with my clients discovering since it shows that one of my hobbies is being handy and I had a good time creating a thoughtful solution that can help other car owners. This small project helps me build my professional portfolio as I use it in marketing meetings with clients as an example they can use to help their customers in their videos.

Gmail address steps for success

Once you start applying for jobs outside of college, consider getting a new Gmail address that doesn't include your college's name. This will set you apart as a professional rather than a student (not to mention that access to your student account may expire when you graduate).

Perhaps many years ago you setup an email address that contains your nickname but doesn't sound very professional. Now would be a great time to setup an email address with this format: [First name] + [Last name] @gmail.com or [first name] + [middle initial] + [last name]@gmail.com. Gmail is viewed as an email system used by professionals and will be well received if the address contains a name that clearly identifies you.

You will never grow out of your email address when it contains your full name. However you will quickly grow out of an email address that contains a childhood username. As an example, my childhood email address was Swimmer174@aol.com. As the captain of the high school swim team, this seemed appropriate at the time. However, I have since changed my email address to be more like [First name] + [Last name] @Gmail.com. Not only was my high school email address short-minded, it was also difficult for people to find my email address when they opened a new message and typed in "Josh Ochs" since Swimmer174 wasn't picked up by autosuggest.

It's important to have a clear, professional email address. In high school, this could be one of the best ways to make you stand out from your peers. After high school, having a professional Gmail address will be the norm, so getting on board early will set you apart.

There's no need to email everyone alerting them that you changed your email address. Look carefully in the settings of Gmail and give it permission to log into your old email account automatically so it can download any new messages every day to your new account for free. Then, you can begin replying to everyone with your new address and everything will funnel into your new Gmail address seamlessly.

Learn more about this technique at SafeSmartSocial.com/book.

As an added benefit, when your internship or employer wants to send something to you online, whether it's a presentation, worksheet, product, or document, you can recommend, "Please share it with me using Google Docs. Here's my Gmail account, firstname.lastname@gmail.com." If this address is anything other than a clear description of your identity, then they may frown upon it. They're really going to like being able to contact you through a professional email identity that matches your full name.

Visit SafeSmartSocial.com/book to register this book for free and we will send you videos and key takeaways to help your students use social media to impress colleges and employers.

Key takeaways from this chapter:
- Gone are the days when employers trusted your PDF or Microsoft word resume without looking you up online.
- It's good to have a thick, relevant history on LinkedIn that colleges can discover and point to as your professional home base online.
- Keep in mind that since the printed version of your resume doesn't have a picture on it, and hiring managers probably met you at an on-campus recruiting event with hundreds of other applicants, you need a clear, classy photo of yourself that they can

use to quickly identify you.

- When someone searches for you online, you want to own and control the first page of the search results they see, and since Google Plus is owned by Google, it's a great place to start.
- Once you have your website built, you can add projects, resumes, and volunteer work at least once per month.
- If your security settings are set to friends only, or friends of friends only, consider making a select few of your best pictures public so that your profile is the first to be discovered instead of someone else's by mistake.
- It's important to have a clear, professional email address. You will never grow out of your email address when it contains your full name.
- Consider creating a clear and concise bio that puts your best foot forward online (without giving away too much personal information).

CHAPTER SIX

How and when to privatize your image

Planning is bringing the future into the present so that you can do something about it now. – Alan Lakein

---

The goal of this chapter is to show you when it's acceptable to privatize your online profiles and when it might look sneaky. It turns out that colleges and employers want to find you online. If you hide your online image an employer will keep researching as they want to find more about you. Colleges and employers are very good at locating (and they use various tools) that help them paint a complete picture of someone. They aren't new to this. We will give you some tips that help you to stay secure, but also have a discoverable presence online.

In a previous chapter we discussed mistakes others make that keep them from having a clean online image. This chapter will focus on mostly helping you stay safe by giving you examples of how much you privatize your online image. The main idea is that you should be careful with sharing personally identifiable information online.

What is Personally Identifiable Information (PII)?

PII is any information people can use to locate your whereabouts, age, patterns, schedule or appearance. We are going to show you how sharing too much PII can make your life less secure.

If you include in your public social media posts your: home address, birthday + age (or year of birth), anything that contains the name of your password (like the name of your dog or cat), or your middle name, then you are sharing Personally Identifiable Information online.

More in depth information could include your opinions of teachers or your school. With that information, anyone could find out where you live and certain people could find out what you are studying, or what year of school you are in. The name of your school can alert someone exactly where you are during school hours.

Another thing that could get you in trouble is sharing when you and your family are going on vacation. That makes it very clear that no one is at home to take care of the house.

Tactical Tip: Taking a lot of photos on your vacation? Consider waiting until you get home before posting a picture of the trip. A possible message could look like this: "We had a great time last week in Hawaii on the Big Island. Here's a pic of us watching the waves."

I don't know why people are so keen to put the details of their private life in public; they forget that invisibility is a superpower.

- Banksy

Also, if your parents or family regularly travel for work or you are at home by yourself several days of the week, don't mention their travel schedule online. It's better to text your BFF and or closest friends about your family schedules. Consider not sharing it online since you're really telling everyone in your network (and possibly their contacts, or the public) exactly when your family will be out of town (or the kids are home alone).

Would you stand up at a coffee shop and yell out your home address?

Pretend that your social media posts are similar to being at a coffee shop having a conversation with your friends while dozens of interested people are listening in. Do you want everyone to know where you live? Do you want the coffee shop people to know when you're traveling? Do you want strangers knowing that you are home alone? Lots of people (that will not comment) can see your post, and most of them are people you do not know. If you wouldn't yell it out at a coffee shop, then it probably doesn't belong on your public profile.

Are you comfortable with all your online friends meeting your parents?

Another part of keeping your online image private is deciding with whom you feel comfortable knowing where you live. To begin, the best online friends are those who you feel totally comfortable letting them come over for dinner to meet your family and/or parents (or maybe they already know your parents). If you're in the gray area and don't know if your parents or family would approve of them, then be careful before accepting them as your "friend" online since they can see all of your information. Make sure you know who they are in real life and are ok with your family meeting them.

Along the same lines, consider everything that you post and ask yourself, "Am I ok with my parents, friends, and future employers seeing this?" Facebook reminds us in their safety guide: "Also remember that any information you post – whether in a comment, a note, or a video chat – might be copied, pasted, and distributed in ways that you didn't intend. Before you post, ask yourself – would I be OK if this content was shared widely at school or with my future employer?"

Search for yourself online each month

Check what information is online about you each month. There is an easy way to see what other people see when they search for you. Google and Bing are incredibly powerful search engines that tailor their searches to each individual person's online preferences. Since Google owns Gmail, it can track what you search for and has access to all of your search history.

When you google yourself while logged into Gmail, your results are tainted by the preferences that Google has recorded for you. To fix that, you need to logout of all Google, Gmail and

LIGHT, BRIGHT AND POLITE®

Google Plus related services before you search yourself. This can take several minutes and be very annoying if you forget your password to get back in.

Wouldn't it be nice if you could open a new browser window that temporarily (only in that window) allowed you to search the web in a logged out "stealth mode." This browser feature is available and it's called Incognito or Private Browsing (depending on which browser you use).

In Google Chrome, you can enter incognito mode by clicking on the menu button found at the top of the screen on the right side. Click "New Incognito Window" to start a new temporary "stealth mode" experience and remove your search-engine bias results to more accurately view Google's native results (what others see about you).

To watch an instructional video on this feature, please visit SafeSmartSocial.com/book

How do you find out when something new online appears in search results?

Next, you can use Google Alerts to have your search results tracked and sent to you each month. As a tip, put your name in quotes. So, if someone mentions you, you will only get the results for "Josh Ochs" not "Josh" or "Ochs." This narrows down your search results to (hopefully) just you.

Another great tool is Mention.net which more accurately searches social media and blogs. It cost less than $10 per month, but it provides more robust results than Google Alerts. Everything about your search that's online can be sent directly to your inbox and is customizable. I personally pay for this service and use it to monitor my image and that of my clients. When you register this book at SafeSmartSocial.com/book you'll get a free trial of Mention.com.

Do you understand how social media companies make money?

It takes a lot of money to run a huge social networking

site, like Facebook or LinkedIn. Have you ever wondered how these companies pay their designers, marketers, and other employees if their service is offered for free?

Caroline Knorr from Common Sense Media encourages parents and students to have this conversation with each other. She says to talk about how social media companies make money. Discuss how social networking companies make money off of 'free services.' Make it clear that every interaction you have with a site provides the company with user data (where you've clicked, what you've clicked on, what you've "liked," who's in your network, etc.). Discuss the value of that information to companies, and how companies peddle that information to other companies. It's important for kids to be informed consumers of the products and services they use, and social media companies are not always transparent about the business arrangement users are entering into when they sign up. If you help your kids to view media critically, they may be less inclined to misuse it."

Should you use a fake name or completely hide my profile from admissions/HR?

A lot of people say that they've totally hidden their Facebook profile (or created a fake name) so that colleges and employers can't find them in search results. They act as though they have outsmarted colleges and employers, but I believe this is hurting them in the long run. Admissions offers and HR departments would rather find your account early on instead of having to keep searching. Many times they will mistake someone else's profile for yours (which might contain even worse photos than yours). You're putting your future in the fate of the search results and in someone else's Facebook page. Why not keep your identity clean and make sure it's easy to stumble upon, and make it something that you're proud of having discovered?

What should you post on Facebook to help yourself stand out?

You may consider finding the most engaging/positive 15-20 pictures that are on your Facebook profile and make those specifically available to the public. One of them should be your profile picture and it should be the same picture that you use as profile pictures on all of your forms of social media, including LinkedIn. Make sure your photos are positive, sincere and easy for someone to recognize you in. You want people to see the photos that give you a really good image and provide a well-rounded reputation. They could be group photos of you volunteering, a group photo of you at a networking event (tasteful and smiling), in a group project, or traveling. Whatever the photos are, run them by a friend and make sure you're putting your best foot forward. Then make them public because you want to get discovered and stand out from the crowded online search results. A little bit of publicity in a Light, Bright, and Polite® manner can be very good.

Facebook includes the following tip to parents of teens and tweens:

Facebook enables people to control the audience of their posts. Encourage your kids to review their privacy settings and to make sure they consider the audience when sharing content on Facebook. Also encourage your kids to use their Activity Log, a powerful tool that enables people to review and manage what they've shared on Facebook. With your activity log, you can manage who sees your content across Facebook. No one else sees your activity log.

This is a safe tool to use to see what you have put out there, going back to when you first opened your Facebook profile. Review your activity log to make sure than only the information you want out there is out there and remove everything else.

Tactical Tip: Once you've made some of your photos public, consider using incognito/private browsing to view your profile with more organic search results (as an outsider). Scroll through all of the tabs at the top of the search engine to look at the photos and videos.

What networks should you privatize?

Facebook should mainly be private. Step back first, though, and make sure that everything you are posting is Light, Bright, and Polite®, whether it is public or not. You can't hide bad behavior. You could hide, however, some of your images, so that they don't get geotagged and people can't see where you live. Privatizing your Facebook page isn't going to help you hide any bad decisions you make online. It will only help to keep your personally identifiable information from spreading.

Twitter is not designed to be a private network. If you try to privatize your tweets, an employer is going to want to know what you are trying to keep secret, that's because Twitter is meant as a public place to share short thoughts and news.

Instagram, on the other hand, may be privatized because it shares so many photos and personally identifiable information. Make sure that you know everyone that follows you. Also, your followers can share your links from Instagram onto other networks. If they tweet your links with your name in them, it makes your information available in search results. On every network it's a good idea to live a life that's Light, Bright, and Polite® (in case something goes wrong).

LinkedIn is a public, professional network that can lead

> Once you've made some of your photos public, consider using incognito/private browsing to view your profile with more organic search results (as an outsider). Scroll through all of the tabs at the top of the search engine to look at the photos and videos.

to you getting a better career. Everything that you have on LinkedIn should be public so that people can see your entire portfolio. Everything on LinkedIn should be 100% Light, Bright, and Polite® and professional. If you feel comfortable, consider posting most of your projects on there. Don't put anything on there that you wouldn't be proud to show off. Also, try to balance your professional image with giving out too much personally identifiable information. The parts of LinkedIn you should hide (or not fill in at all) are the areas where it asks for your birth date and your relationship status. These are two parts of LinkedIn that (in my opinion) should not be a part of your public resume. This information has nothing to do with whether you're a good candidate at a college or for a job.

> *Everything secret degenerates, even the administration of justice; nothing is safe that does not show how it can bear discussion and publicity.*
> - Lord Acton

Should your blog be public?

Blogs are meant to be found on Google, so yes, you should consider always making your blog public. It should always contain content that helps others in a way that you're proud of and is very easy to agree with (not dramatic or controversial). You can learn more about my blog at JoshOchs.com to see how I share short blurbs of my travels and experiences to better shape my search results.

Symantec Privacy Tips

Satnam Narang is one of the leading online security experts at Symantec and he gives us some great insight to being safe online. Here's some of Satnam's tips for protecting your social accounts:

It's a social world

The most dominating force on the Internet today is social. Right now, I have friends pinning their wedding ideas, instagramming lattes, snapchatting outfits, checking into restaurants on Foursquare, Vining videos of their cats, sharing newborn baby photos on Facebook, and tweeting in anticipation of Their favorite show's premiere. As these services become more and more popular, they are targeted more frequently by scams, spam, and phishing attempts.

Know your settings

Symantec Security Response advises social users to familiarize themselves with the privacy settings and security services offered by each of these social networks and applications.

1. **Public or private?** By default, many of these services encourage you to share updates publicly. Most offer privacy as a global setting to make your profile public or private, while some offer more options, allowing you to make individual posts public or private. Make sure you review these settings before posting to these services.

2. **Strong passwords and password reuse.** Use a strong password for each service and be sure not to reuse passwords across your social networks.

3. **If available, set up two-factor authentication.** Some services like Facebook and Twitter offer two-factor authentication as an added measure of security for your account. Normally, to login to a service, you input a password, which is something you know. Using two-factor authentication introduces something you have, usually in the form of a randomly generated number or token that can be delivered to your phone through SMS or a number generator within the services' mobile application. This way, if your password is compromised, the thief will need access to your SMS/text messages before they can login.

Know your enemy

The biggest enemies of most social networking and

application users are the spammers and scammers that want to hijack your social accounts to peddle spam, convince you to fill out surveys, or install applications.

1. **Free stuff is not free**. Many scammers will try to entice you with the idea that you can win free gadgets or gift cards if you fill out a survey, install an application, or share a post on your social network. It just isn't that easy and by doing so, you could give away your personal information.

2. **Want more followers and likes?** There is always a price to pay for trying to get more followers and likes. Whether that's paying money for fake followers and likes or willingly giving up your account credentials and becoming part of a social botnet. These schemes aren't worth it.

3. **Trending topics are ripe for abuse.** Whether it's sporting events or pop stars, the death of celebrities, popular television season or series finales, or the newest gadget announcement, scammers and spammers know what's popular and will find a way to insert themselves into the conversation to trick users into doing their bidding. Know that this is inevitable and think twice before blindly clicking on links.

4. **Is this picture or video of you?** These scammers want your password and they'll attempt to convince you to unknowingly give it to them. This is called phishing. If you click on a link and it takes you to a webpage that looks like a login page for a social networking service, don't just type in your password. Check the address bar to make sure it's not some long URL that has the word Twitter or Facebook in it. Open up a new browser tab and manually type in twitter.com or facebook.com to see if you're still logged in. More often than not, you probably are.

All of these tips are important in keeping your personal information safe. Many people keep their information online (like their middle name, phone number, or birthday) but do not make it public. If someone was able to break into their account, though, they would have all of that information. It could be used to do many things, even apply for credit cards in your name, without you knowing about it.

It's ok to ask people to remove online photos of you

Kim Sanchez's final word of advice as the former Director of Online Safety & Accessibility at Microsoft talks about restoring your online reputation. She says, "If you find information about yourself that does not fit the reputation you want, act quickly. In a respectful way, ask the person who posted it to remove it or correct an error. If you feel a public correction is necessary, present your case simply and politely." There is no sense in leaving harmful or untrue information about you on the internet. Make sure that you are protecting yourself and your reputation."

Let people discover you online so that you can put your best foot forward. Make sure that when you google yourself, what you discover is awesome.

Visit SafeSmartSocial.com/book to register this book for free and we will send you videos and key takeaways to help your students use social media to impress colleges and employers.

Key takeaways from this chapter:

- Taking a lot of photos on your vacation? Consider waiting until you get home before posting a picture of the trip.
- Your posts are like buttons on an elevator. Each of your posts either take you up or they take you down.
- Consider everything that you post and ask yourself, "Am I ok with my parents, friends, and future employers seeing this?"

- Search for yourself online each month on Google.
- When you Google yourself while logged into Gmail, your results are tainted by the preferences that Google has recorded for you.
- You may consider finding the most engaging/positive 15-20 pictures that are on your Facebook profile and make those specifically available to the public.
- Once you've made some of your photos public, consider using incognito/private browsing to view your profile with more organic search results (to view your profile in the public's view).
- The most dominating force on the Internet today is social media.
- It's ok to ask people to remove online photos of you.

CHAPTER SEVEN
How to talk to your kids

Instead of worrying about what people say of you, why not spend time trying to accomplish something they will admire. – Dale Carnegie

---

If we tell young kids, "Don't touch the stove," guess what they want to do? Touch the stove. Or, if we scare them enough, they will develop anxiety and fear about the stove which might cause them to avoid it for years. We don't want to create either of these responses. If we instead teach them about cooking and how the stove helps to heat the pan to cook the food, they will better understand how the stove is used for good, and why it can be very painful to touch while hot. This approach demystifies the stove, and neutralizes emotions surrounding the stove so that it's no longer tempting or anxiety-provoking.

We use this approach to show kids that social media is a great tool they can use to put their best foot forward. Just like a stove, it can also burn you. But when it's used right, it can help you cook a delicious meal, metaphorically speaking.

Tshaka Armstrong, FOX 11 reporter, technology expert, and the President and CEO of Digital Shepherds, recommends,

> Start when they're young. Not just with social media, but technology in general. Normalize the use of tech and social media in your home so that it isn't odd for the children to have you involved in their 'online lives.'

Things always get tough and you'll generally experience 'push back' if you wait until later to interject your wisdom and advice, so the earlier the better and be consistent!"

Excellent advice.

Parents, be careful when telling your kids what is bad on social media

Kids have been told that social media can be harmful, but not necessarily how it can harm them, or why they should care. If directives don't make sense, kids will disregard them, thinking that adults don't understand things in which they don't even widely participate. This naïvité can hurt their online image, because they might do something that parents understand to be unwise, or hide the bad behavior from their parents, not knowing that it's hurting them in the long run.

One of the biggest issues here is that parents don't alert their kids ahead of time what's wrong to do on social media. Or, if they do, it's a generic reprimand like, "Don't say anything negative, everything is public." Instead, consider having a dialog with our kids about what's on social media. Make sure that they are sharing their information with you.

Consider having a dialog before your kids ever get their phone. It could start a little something like this: "Since I purchased this phone, I'm loaning it to you under these conditions. You must be friends with me on every app that you download (then list them out) and I can have this phone back any day I want it. " Then, when you see something that's troubling you can say, "Remember you're borrowing my phone that I bought for you, let's talk about the rules again."

> *Nine tenths of education is encouragement.*
> – Anatole France

One way to use positive psychology to get good results from kids in their social media behavior is to motivate them to want to impress the right people before they post things online.

Facebook includes the following advice in their Online Safety Guide:

One of the best ways to begin a conversation is to ask your teens why services like Facebook are important to them. You might also ask them to show you how to set up your own Facebook timeline, so you can see what it's all about. Discuss what's appropriate information to share online—and what isn't.

When you are having this conversation with your child, don't forget to put an emphasis on working with them and not against them. You could sit down with your kid and ask them to walk you through their Facebook, Twitter, or Instagram accounts. Have them teach you all about that social media platform so that they can feel like they are the expert at something. Ask them how they decide who to follow and why, how they decide what to post and why. Inevitably, there will be something that they have posted, or something that one of their friends have posted to their page, that will make them uncomfortable for you to see. Anything they cringe at showing you probably shouldn't be on their account in the first place, but can be a great place to continue the conversation about how they can shine online.

Parents can start a conversation that shows their kids that being LBP can make them more popular through a clean online reputation. Sometimes it's hard to connect with our kids, or know how to say things in a way that they will understand, but it's very important for us to make it understandable on their level. **When working with kids, consider avoiding the use of these buzz terms that were created by Fortune500 marketing departments: "digital citizen" and "digital literacy."** These words aren't a part of the usual middle school or high school level conversation, and they are not going to resonate with teenagers based on their current experiences.

Caroline Knorr, Parenting Editor at Common Sense Media, offers some advice to parents on how to start a conversation with their kid about shining online:

Talk—and listen—to your kids. They might tell you everything you want to know or at least drop the name of an app or a website you can check out on your own. Even if you can't stay on top of every new thing that comes along, concentrate your efforts on keeping the lines of communication open so kids will come to you if a problem arises. Make sure kids know it's OK to make mistakes and that they don't need to hide these from you — that you can actually help them through tough spots.

Talk about personal privacy. The word "privacy" means different things to different people. Privacy settings let you keep certain details hidden from contacts on your social network, as well as from the social networking company itself. It's interesting to discuss your family's values about personal privacy. What information should be kept private from other people? What privacy settings do your kids use? Which ones are important? Have they ever gone back and deleted or edited old posts so their new friends wouldn't see them? What information would they NOT want potential colleges, employers, coaches, or other authority figures to see?

Ask which apps and sites are popular with your kids' friends. Kids may open up more when they're talking about someone else. Ask if your kids use the apps and sites that their friends use. Are you missing out on valuable information about your kids if you don't have the latest apps on your phone?

Ask kids what they think is inappropriate on social networks. A lot of times kids are just trying to be funny or get attention when they misbehave online. They may inadvertently hurt someone else's feelings or share something that they themselves are embarrassed by. Ask your kids if they have ever seen others do things that they would regret. Have they ever seen someone bully someone else online? What did they do? What would they do if they witnessed it? Would they have the confidence to share it with an adult?

Share what you're using and model the behavior you want your kids to emulate. Show them your Facebook page, favorite videos, or a game you're obsessed with. They may be inspired to reciprocate. Remember that you are your kids' digital role model. They will learn from you how to conduct themselves, how to set limits, how to respect their friends' privacy, and how to know when to put all the digital tools away and just focus on what's happening in front of them.

> *Education is the most powerful weapon which you can use to change the world.*
> – Nelson Mandela

If you feel intimidated talking to your kid about these social media applications, here's how you can first get a handle on how to use them:

First, you can just research the app you want to talk to your kid about using Google or Bing. Click on the "video" button at the top of the search box to learn how the app works. There is so much information online that you can find in less than 10 minutes.

Second, you can visit SafeSmartSocial.com, and watch free videos to learn about the apps.

Third, get your kids involved by asking them to teach you how the app works. Once you've got the basic idea of what the app does, you can "play dumb" and ask your kids to explain it to you in more detail. Kids love feeling like the expert and you will learn about the app in their terms, which will help you relate to them even more.

Tactical Tip: When learning something new from a kid, try not to say "Why would I want to do that?" instead say "Cool, what happens when I do that?" When parents ask "why" when learning, it tends to make them sound out of touch.

Fourth, if you see your kids posting on a new app, ask them to walk you through their online profile and their most recent seven posts. Ask them about some of the photos and have them explain how they think others would perceive that photo. Let them take the driver's seat in this exercise so that they feel comfortable. When they describe the photo it makes them take ownership of the images and they sometimes will self-correct and see what you see (without you having to seem negative).

Unlike 20 years ago, today, kids want you to read their diary. Social media has become the new diary for kids. Decades ago, my sisters used to say, "Don't read my diary!" Tweens and teens have become accustomed to sharing their selfies for everyone to see. They get some sort of thrill out of sharing their innermost secrets online that elicit a response. In many cases, kids are better at engaging their followers than many of the Fortune500 brands that I've been speaking to over the last decade. Kids these days are good at sharing their online "diary" because they like the instant feedback it gives them. These apps reward those that share secrets.

When learning something new from a kid, try not to say "Why would I want to do that?" instead say "Cool, what happens when I do that?"

Nowadays there isn't any sneaking around to find (and read) a kid's diary. Instead, kids post their most private moments on their social media accounts for everyone to see (or for a college to eventually find). All a parent needs to do is "friend" their kid online, become an observer and read all of their kid's posts and tweets. So, to keep your "diary reading privileges" intact, consider not commenting directly on your kid's posts. Instead, use those posts to start a dialog around those issues and topics with your kids in real life (maybe around the dinner table).

Find someone you trust to talk with your kids

If you are having a hard time connecting with your kid on this topic, consider that you might not be the best fit for the job right now. It may be that there's another parent (who you trust) who can talk to your kids about being safe and putting their best foot forward. Or, you can use one of your adult friends, someone who your kid knows and you trust, and this person can have a meaningful conversation with them about social media. Also consider other people in your family who might have more knowledge on the topic. You could use a "cool" favorite aunt or uncle. I hope to someday be this "cool uncle" to my nieces and nephews. :)

To keep your "diary reading privileges" intact, consider not commenting directly on kid's posts. Instead, use those posts to start a dialog around those issues and topics with your kids in real life (maybe around the dinner table).

Whoever is talking to your kids, start by setting some goals. Have an important talk about which colleges and/or careers most excite them. By talking about long term goals and organizations, kids will start to understand their long term picture. Then, ask your kids what types of online posts and photos might impress those colleges and/or employers. In general, talk with your kids about keeping their online image Light, Bright, and Polite® to impress these groups in the future.

Many organizations will use the term "digital citizenship" to describe the way kids should interact positively online. I believe this phrase is difficult to understand for most kids.

Here's my rough formula for Digital Citizenship:

> **Be Active:**
> Post something weekly
> +
> **Be Kind:**
> Post only Light, Bright and Polite® content that is less about you and more about activities and others
> +
> **Be Long Term:**
> Ask yourself, "Will I be proud of this in five years?"

What if I'm not friends with my kids online?

If possible, try to become friends with your kids on social media. Some kids won't want to be friends with their parents on social media. However, if the parent is buying the device, many will tell you that they get total control over the experience. Also, keep in mind you're probably paying the bill. Many people say that if the parent buys the car and pays for insurance, then they get to take the keys any time. Some would say that goes for the cell phone too. Many social networks won't allow you to see what your kids are posting if you're not a friend/follower (if their profiles are set to private).

How do you motivate your kids to care?

To start, pick a long term goal that your kid has. You could start a conversation like this, "You love football. Wouldn't it be nice if you could play college football at Stanford? To do that, you need to impress Coach Smith with your social media. What kinds of posts do you think Coach Smith might like to see?" This puts their social media usage into an entirely new perspective. Now, instead of just thinking about whether you or their friends like their posts, your kids are thinking long term about how other people like teachers, coaches, and employers like their posts.

What if my kid makes an online mistake?

At some point, your kid is probably going to slip up. That happens to everyone. If you see bad posts, consider not scolding your kids over that specific post, but rather asking yourself, "Why did my kid post this? What can I learn from this? How can I respond to this by starting a dialog with my kids?" The best place to start is trying to understand why it happened, then working on making sure it doesn't happen again on a public social network. Maybe your kid didn't realize it was a bad thing to put online, or maybe they need a gentle reminder that this doesn't fit into their long term image plan/goal. If you just scold, they won't learn what they did wrong and will just try to shield you from their behavior. Every kid is different, so they each have different needs. The goal is to not try and make them perfect online, but instead help them with the process of shining online over the long term.

> *The most influential of all educational factors is the conversation in a child's home.*
> -William Temple

Use celebrities to make a point

Here's a fun game to play with your kids. Use a search engine to find all different kinds of famous people. There are celebrities who are famous for being rich and successful, and some who are more infamous, because of dramatic actions they have taken to get attention online. Consider the differences between Steve Jobs and the Kardashians. Ask your kids who they would rather be. What lasting imprint do they want to leave? What is their "brand," or their reputation, going to say about them? Do they want to be the inventor of the iPhone or be known for sharing all of their most personal details in a dramatic TV show where people lose respect for them?

No matter how you decide to talk with your kids about their social media presence, make sure it's one that they are proud of in five years as they grow up. Make sure your social media approach with them is one that helps them to interact with their friends in a quality manner and also strengthens your relationship with them as you walk down this new digital road as their parent. It's ok to be firm in your decisions, just make sure you keep the lines of communication open to understand why your kids behave online in the way they do.

Visit SafeSmartSocial.com/book to register this book for free and we will send you videos and key takeaways to help your students use social media to impress colleges and employers.

Key takeaways from this chapter:

- Be explanatory with your kids about the problems with social media. Give context to how it can harm them. Just creating rules without context can lead to rebellion. Think: Dialog.
- Have your kids walk you through their social media accounts teaching you what they're about and who they follow and why.
- Research social media applications by googling them before talking to your kid, if you're worried about sounding out of the loop
- Find someone you trust to talk to your kid, if your relationship is strained or if either of you find the conversation awkward.
- Try to become friends with your kid on social media, but don't comment on their posts.
- Find a goal that motivates them, like playing football for a college team. Help them create an image to help them achieve that goal.
- If your kid makes a mistake on social media, spend more time trying to learn why than making them feel bad.
- Analyze celebrity social media game to decide together what seems praiseworthy and what doesn't.

CHAPTER EIGHT
How to make a plan together

Instead of worrying about what people say of you, why not spend time trying to accomplish something they will admire. – Dale Carnegie

---

Marcus Buckingham is a bestselling HR and leadership author, and someone for whom I once worked. This is how I know his excellence at studying leadership and creating formulas others can follow. After studying thousands of interviews, here is his tip on providing focus to build better leaders:

"Define excellence vividly, quantitatively. Paint a picture for your most talented employees of what excellence looks like. Keep everyone pushing and pushing toward the right-hand edge of the bell curve."

Although you're not running a company, this can work with kids. To excel, you must know what your goal is, define it and illustrate it in your kid's mind, and then find out how to work towards it. You won't complete your objectives until you define the direction that you need to move. Showing your kid who they need to impress, and how, will give them some direction of what to do when social media pressure kicks in.

The greatest gifts you can give your children are the roots of responsibility and the wings of independence.
- Denis Waitley

Who is your kid going to want to impress in the next few years? Start with your target audience.

Is it a college? If so, consider making a list of colleges that your kid (and/or you) want to impress. Take the best school in the list and:

1) **Find the name of one of the admissions officers and make them a role model for your kids.** People respond well to having a physical example to look towards instead of just an idea. For example, let's say that your kid wants to go to school at USC. You can can look up their admissions officers. Perhaps one of them is named Bill Smith. Perhaps you can talk with your kid and remind them to consider before each post to ask themselves, "Will Bill Smith approve, disapprove or not care about this post?" If he's going to disapprove or not care, then it's probably not helping your kid's online image (and perhaps could hurt them). Anything that isn't adding value to your online image is considered "off topic" and can take away from your online focus. More on this later.

2) **Google the name of the school and find out what programs they are known for**. Write these down and incorporate those items into your plan. Example: UCLA might have a great cooking team and your kid is really good at cooking. It's not about dictating what your child participates in, but instead encouraging them in whatever they're good at. Consider connecting the dots between the offerings of their dream school and what your child is good at, then highlighting those areas. Once you know the similarities, talk with your kids about ways to integrate those similarities into their pastimes and encourage them to post those things on social media.

3) **Find the name(s) of some students at the school who are leaders on campus.** These are easy to find because they usually come up in Google results when you research the school. These may be the valedictorian or the extracurricular volunteers, current students or recent students. Write their name down and google them to learn more about their online

portfolio of accomplishments. Don't get creepy, but use their Google results with your kids as an example of what that school looks for in a leader. Again, kids respond well to real examples (and we have an example from Harvard at the end of this book). Choose students a few years older and involved in activities your child may aspire to participate in.

Tactical Tip: Parents, you want to look at the role models this ahead of time and make sure there are no red cups in their online image. That might not make this process very wholesome if the example has a lot of party pics (when you've been talking them up).

After researching these items on your own, decide which you'll share with your kids. While you're doing that, be sure to encourage the importance of this method. If you do all of the work, and they don't feel as though they have a stake in the process, this method won't stick with them. Your kids need to want to find this interesting and this planning for the future will help guide them to be smart online.

Ask your kids to ask themselves what to highlight online. Circle below at least one from each category to focus

WARNING (beware before you post any of these)
- Bringing awareness to a topic that may be political in nature (not a good topic if it is related to politics and/ or emotional and/or religious).
- Politics
- Religion
- Defaming other people (like other schools, sport teams, bad customer service at restaurants you may have visited, etc.)
- Posting in a passionate manner to build support for a new cause that hasn't proven itself for more than a decade.

Light (helping others)
- Volunteering
- Donating time
- Helping to build something

Bright (teaching and sharing)
- Inspiring others
- Sharing your hobby (cooking or crafts)
- Learning a new language

Polite (being a team player)
- Sports
- Music
- On campus clubs

Now that we know on which positive areas you want to focus, it will encourage you to keep thinking about them. Even in areas that you didn't circle, ask your kids to keep everything Light, Bright and Polite® before they post. And be careful to stay away from the warning/beware column.

> One of the quickest ways to find issues is to Google/Bing your name and click on the "images" button to get a visual representation of your online presence.

Later in the book, we'll teach you how to test your long-term image plan with a couple simple online search tips to determine how effective you are.

Tactical Tip: One of the quickest ways to find issues is to Google/Bing your name and click on the "images" button to get a visual representation of your online presence.

In 2013, there was a New York teen, Kwasi Enin, who gained acceptance into all eight of the Ivy League schools (Brown University, Columbia University, Cornell University, Dartmouth College, Harvard University, Princeton University,

Yale University, and the University of Pennsylvania). Apparently, his whole life his parents held his academics to a high standard, which really paid off in the end. He was also very active, playing an instrument, singing in the school choir, and playing a sport. He shows that being a well-rounded student, with academics and extracurricular activities, is a great way to stand out.[1]

Enin's admission essay focused on how music has played a big role in his life. It's important, while kids are busy with their daily activities that they to remember to focus on a few good things, not a bunch of mediocre things. The quality of the things you do, not the quantity, is what's really important. Encourage your kids to be well-rounded and professional.

What does your kid's personal reputation say about your their next project?

Look at your kid's personal brand (their reputation) as an investment: Their online image and personal reputation has the potential to last longer than your own lifespan. While the projects they are working on might grow or be shot down, their personal reputation will remain and (if they are careful) add value to each new stage of their career. Colleges (and future employers) will follow your kid's reputation from project to project if they feel comfortable with it. When your kids launch new projects, their personal reputation has the potential to guarantee they never have to start from scratch again. If your kid considers him- or herself to be someone who is focused on the long term, whether it's a sport, hobby, or university, a good personal reputation is an invaluable investment.

This is a great time to create a plan to protect your kid's online reputation and build their personal brand. Their

---

1. Ray Sanchez and Sheila Steffen, "NY student accepted to all 8 Ivy League colleges picks Yale," *CNN.com*, last modified May 1, 2014, SafeSmartSocial.com/research.

'personal brand' involves everything they are posting for people to see, so it's an extension of their reputation. Whether you realize it or not, your kids are always being evaluated on their personal brand. That's how people assess others.

An applicant's chance of getting accepted is hindered when a recruiter discovers something negative about them on social media. On the flip side, recruiters react very favorably to posts and tweets about volunteering and considering how what you do now will affect your kid's image in the future.

Short-term thinking brings long-term reputation issues (that may harm your kid's online image).

The University of Liverpool, like many universities, puts out a guide on how to use social media in a way that won't disqualify you from their admission. Some of the guidelines are general, but below are a few key tips taken directly from their Social Media Compliance Policy. This will give you an idea of what colleges are actually thinking about social media:

1. **Consider your message, audience and goals.** Don't forget that it's very difficult to limit who sees what on social media, so bear that in mind before posting content.
2. **Be accurate**. Mistakes can happen, but try to make sure what you post is accurate.
3. **Consider the impact.** Material posted on social media can have a long-term impact on your employability prospects and reputation. Make sure you consider the consequences before you post.
4. **Respect others' privacy.** Don't include personal information about yourself or others including other students and University staff. Familiarize yourself with professionalism and confidentiality rules – make sure you know the rules to protect privacy relating to your area of study at the University. For example, Health Sciences, Dentistry, Medical and Veterinary

students must retain professionalism and respect confidentiality in clinical cases. Research students must also be aware of rules governing the recruitment of study volunteers.

5. **Be aware of copyright and intellectual property issues.** Do you need permission to publish the information on your page? Make sure you check before posting because infringement of rules could lead to legal action.

6. **Don't use the University logo.** The University logo and any other university images or icons must not be used for personal social media sites.

7. **Social media**. Social media use — from personal or University accounts — is monitored by the University and covered by regulations governing student conduct. Inappropriate social media use (for example: offensive, intimidating, threatening, indecent or illegal content) is likely to result in students being referred to the University's student disciplinary procedures.

Universities aren't trying to hide that they monitor social media. They don't want to trick you, but if you are an affiliated member they don't want you putting hateful, inappropriate things online. Ultimately, it will look bad on them for being associated with you at all. With that in mind, don't give them reasons to not want you to be a part of their team.

Even though the future seems far away, it is actually beginning right now. –Mattie Stepanek

Kim Sanchez, former Director Online Safety and Accessibility for Microsoft Corporation, gives more advice on the matter. Her next tip towards taking charge of your online reputation is to cultivate your professional reputation. Kim says,

Publish the positive. Create what you want others to see. Link anything you publish to your name. Add your comments on career-oriented blogs and participate in online forums where you have expertise. Carefully consider adding any personal information to your professional profile and only do so in a way that will reflect well on that image.

Employers and colleges will eventually find any personal profiles you have, even if your kid uses different email addresses and/or usernames. Make sure your kid's online presence is a "family oriented" version of what their professional profile should be. Want to stand out? Have them add some wholesome content to their professional profile so it makes them stand out from peers. These could be volunteer photos or travel experiences that make them more well-rounded.

Do right. Do your best. Treat others as you want to be treated. - Lou Holtz

Create a social media agreement/contract with your kids

Another tip that would really help you to get ahead of the curve is to create a social media agreement with your kids.

Robyn Spoto is the co-founder of the MamaBear app and she has these suggestions:

1. Create a smartphone and/or social media contract with your children.

2. A great first step is to have a conversation about boundaries and create a written agreement – a contract with your child. Then, be sure to check out parental restrictions offered on most devices on the market.

3. My favorite points to include in a family cell phone contract are:

a. If I drop my phone or damage it in any way, I am responsible for repairing or replacing it.

b. I will always answer the phone when my parents or siblings call and I will respond to family texts as soon as I get them.

c. I will not use my phone at the dinner table or at family events.

4. To get a full social media contract emailed to you, visit SafeSmartSocial.com/book.

Visit SafeSmartSocial.com/book to register this book for free and we will send you videos and key takeaways to help your students use social media to impress colleges and employers.

Key takeaways from this chapter:

· Show WHY kids should participate in having a clean online presence, not just to tell them that having a negative one is bad. Remember, the ultimate goal is to impress colleges and employers.
· Normalize the use of tech and social in your home so that it isn't odd for the children to have you involved in their "online lives. It's not always about teaching your kids every little thing, as much as it is about motivating your family to want to use social media in a smart way.
· When learning something new from a kid, try not to say "Why would I want to do that?" instead say "Cool, what happens when I do that?"
· Consider not commenting directly on kid's posts. Instead, use those posts to start a dialog around those issues and topics with your kids in real life (maybe

around the dinner table).

- If you are having a hard time connecting with your kids, consider that you might not be the best fit for the job right now. It may be that there's another parent (that you trust) who can talk to your kids about being safe and putting their best foot forward.
- Ask your kids to think: "before I post this, will it help me get into college?"
- It's not about dictating what your child participates in, but instead encouraging them in whatever they're good at.
- Ask yourself: What do I want to be known for? Then share that subject on social media.
- One of the quickest ways to find issues is to Google your name and click on the "images" button to get a visual representation of your online presence.
- Remember to focus on a few good topics to share. The quality of the posts and topics you share (not the quantity) is what's really important.
- Create a plan to protect your online reputation and create your personal brand.
- Look at your personal brand (your reputation) as an investment: your online image and personal reputation has the potential to last longer than your own lifespan.
- Short-term thinking brings long-term reputation issues (that may harm your kid's online image).
- Publish the positive. Create what you want others to see. Link anything you publish to your name.
- Carefully consider before adding any personal information to your professional profile and only do so in a way that will reflect well on that image.
- Be active. Be kind. Think long term.

CHAPTER NINE

Case studies from successful students making a difference

A career is born in public, talent in privacy. – Marilyn Munroe

---

Т

he goal of this chapter is to show examples of other kids using social media as a portfolio to highlight their accomplishments. We will outline these individuals and show how they are using LinkedIn, Twitter, Facebook, Instagram or YouTube to share their positive message. These examples will all highlight ways that kids can use social media to impress colleges and employers. Under each example we will highlight a "lesson learned" so kids can gather how they can emulate the role model in their own life on social media.

Since there's so much negativity online, we want to use this chapter to give kids a positive set of ideas they can emulate.

It's important to understand that whatever you do in real life will end up online. So you're going to get caught either in a positive way or a negative way. In these examples, teens and tweens got caught doing great things in real life and they ended up online.

The best online stars are those that are doing meaningful things in real life and letting that dictate how they shine online.

Brendan Craig — 14-year-old Entrepreneur

Los Angeles, CA native Brendan Craig has been a food truck lover since the age of 11 when he first started watching the TV show, The Great Food Truck Race. At that age, he was a shy and reserved boy who was so nervous about talking to people when his parents first took him to a food truck event, that he had his dad ask one of the food truck drivers for their business card. After that, the family frequented other trucks in the area and Brendan always picked up a business card, via his dad or mom.

Brendan realized that he had the potential for a great idea. In his area, food trucks didn't have a lot of online presence. Brendan took the many business cards he had collected and created an Instagram account for people to see where the trucks were and what kinds of food they sold. His account gradually became a success, and grew to over 1,000 followers.

A couple of food truck bloggers in San Francisco found Brendan's Instagram and Twitter accounts and met with Brendan in LA to talk about his work with food trucks. When two aspiring documentary filmmakers approached the bloggers about ideas for doing a documentary on food trucks in LA, the bloggers suggested they meet with Brendan. After talking with Brendan, the filmmakers decided to focus the documentary around him and his love of food trucks. It was a great way to showcase his passion. Brendan was also getting offers to work for individual food trucks, to be their social media manager. At the age of 13, he kindly declined their request, but he has left himself a great path should he choose to pursue it in the future.

It came time for Brendan to apply to a selective private high school in El Segundo, CA. During his interview process, the admission officer asked the usual "Tell me about yourself?" Brendan was able to reply, confidently, "I have my own business." The two engaged in a meaningful conversation about how that influenced Brendan's character and about how it had become his passion. Brendan was able to showcase his talents in a positive way while feeling confident and standing out from his peers.

The interview was a great success and Brendan was accepted to the school. It turns out that out of 75 total students in his class, he is just one of three people to have their own business. The head of the school has since been following Brendan's Twitter page for his food truck updates.

Tactical Tip: This goes to show that: (1) Schools look at your social media, (2) to make a lasting impression in whatever you do, you need to be confident in your ability, passionate, and have a unique angle, and (3) Having a clean online image (like Brendan) is going to add value to any organization that you are considering. They will recognize and appreciate this.

In Brendan's Spanish class his teacher assigned a project for the students to design their own food truck concept for homework. She knew about Brendan's experience in the field and set him up to lead a class presentation about the different kinds of truck concepts and menu items. When he was 11 years old and began collecting food truck business cards via his parents, this would have been an intimidating speech. But now that he had experience with food trucks (and their owners), he was confident in his knowledge and was able to give an incredible presentation to his peers.

In one of the first chapters of one of Dale Carnegie's books, The Keys to Public Speaking, he says, "Anyone can feel comfortable and confident speaking to 1 to 1000 people, if they simply focus on what they do best and are passionate about in the world."

For Brendan, the topic he is most passionate about is food trucks. For other kids it could be something very different. It could be gardening, gaming, Spanish, French, traveling, Wikipedia, etc.

Brendan was also approached by a teacher at school asking him how to book a food truck for her wedding. He is seriously considering combining his similar passion for photography with his blooming food truck business to book and photograph major events for wedding parties, schools, and large organizations. This two prong approach will give him an advantage by adding a lot of value in this unique industry.

Key takeaway: Brendan is focusing on something he is passionate about that also helps other people in a way that is adding so much value, that people can't afford not to work with him. That's what colleges should see in you. They should see you focused on something that you do well, that you want to help others, and that you're refining your approach and to add as much value as possible. Not just telling a story, but actually having traction. Brendan does that because he sees the need for it and that's his passion.

Tanya Shaby – Harvard Law Student

When Tanya applied to Harvard Law School she knew she needed to have more than just a high GPA to impress the admissions department. Having a well-rounded image could add to her resume and show how involved and dedicated she is both in class and outside of school.

In talking with me, she offered some great advice.

First, she said, schools and employers want to see some type of serious commitment in an applicant's life. Tanya used her excellent ice skating skills to show how committed she could be to a project. She took ice skating to a national level and became the president of the California figure skating team. She made her achievements discoverable by starting her own YouTube channel and posting several videos of her in skating practice and at competitions. She put her passion for skating on YouTube to let her real life activities become a part of her online digital footprint. It is important to spend your time on a hobby that you would be proud of ending up online. It is also important to take a leadership role in your hobby so that you can use it to show how dedicated you are to being successful in a subject.

Second, Tanya suggests students should package themselves in such a way that they have more than just a high GPA to show for their efforts. During the application process many of her peers had much better grades than Tanya when applying to law school. Instead of competing on GPA alone, she relied on her essays and resume to package herself and create an interesting, well-rounded story. She used the bigger picture to showcase her hard working personality and emphasize how she would be successful someday as a lawyer with her work ethic. Tanya suggests to students to share their passion and/or hobby online to emphasize their unique story and be more than just a GPA.

Key takeaway: Be well-rounded and discoverable online doing the things you claim to spend time doing. Provide evidence of your successes and excellence.

Bethany Mota — YouTube Celebrity

Bethany Mota is a young 20-something who took to video-blogging on YouTube to escape bullying as a young teenager. In a Business Insider interview, she revealed that, "I didn't want to talk to anyone. I didn't want to leave my house. [YouTube] was kind of an outlet for me to be myself and not really worry about what anyone else thought."

Her approach is inspirational because instead of angrily lashing out at the kids who teased her, and instead of clamming up and retreating from her life, she found something healthy to do with her time: She taught others with her fashion and makeup YouTube videos. Now she is a well-known inspirational blogger who does "motavatours" to meet and interact with her fans. She has a strong YouTube presence that is fun and uplifting, the perfect combination for someone who wishes to stand out positively.

Key takeaway: Find something you can do online that

helps others and gives you a creative outlet to make a positive difference.

Cain Monroe — 9-year-old Entrepreneur

At the age of nine, Cain Monroe was discovered by the Imagination Foundation non-profit for building an elaborate cardboard arcade inside of his father's used auto sales store. The non-profit organization works to promote creativity and entrepreneurship in children. Now, the group holds "cardboard challenges" across the globe for more than 100,000 kids in 50 countries. Cain built something in real life that was so inspirational that he created "5 Lessons for Entrepreneurs." They are: 1) be nice to customers, 2) do a business that is fun, 3) do not give up! (emphasized), 4) start with what you have, and 5) use recycled stuff.

His story is inspiring because even at a young age, he spent his time building something that he was proud to show off online. When his real life project was put online, people quickly realized he had a spark for creativity and a mind for business. His idea, with the help of the Imagination Foundation, has helped spread that spark to countless kids and communities. Growing his idea into such a large event has also had an incredible impact on Caine himself. Apparently, he used to struggle in school, but now that he has been recognized for his unique idea, his grades have flourished and his stutter has diminished.

Key takeaway: Take your real life passion and realize that with some hard work it can end up helping you build a strong online image (that might also inspire others) and will help you shine online.

Mia Goleniowska — 10-year-old Author

Ten-year-old Mia Goleniowska inspired and helped her mother write the book I *Love You Natty: A Sibling's Introduction to Down Syndrome.* When Natty was born, her mother Hayley was searching for books on her genetic condition, especially those she could share with her other daughter, Mia, to explain Natty's experience. She wanted to fill the gap of books written to help families like hers.

Mia played a special role in writing the book. Hayley used Mia's little notes and poems that she wrote to Natty to make up part of the book. Mia and her family's story is inspiring because instead of being distraught over Natty's differences, they have found the joy that Natty brings and shared that special feeling with other families. Mia and Hayley's book is a favorite among others with Down Syndrome kids because everyone can find their family role depicted and every page inspires.

Key takeaway: How you deal with real life struggles can be a great story to inspire others and motivate them with your positive approach.

Ryan Parrilla — Instagram Photographer

Ryan Parrilla is a teenage photographing star. Since a young age he has been interested in taking photos and experimenting with different elements to make them more visually appealing. A few years ago, his parents saw his potential and bought him a Canon DSLR, but told him that he was not allowed to take it out of the house until he learned how to use it. The DSLR is complicated, and he gave up on his photography interest for a little while. When his sister got an iPod, however, that interest was rekindled with the Instagram app.

Now Parrilla has learned how to use his Canon and takes stunning photographs, posting them to his Instagram account. He has 85,000 plus followers, but that wasn't enough for him. He created another website NovessPhoto.com to showcase his talent and share individual pictures. At 15 years old, he has mastered his online presence in a positive way, which will show favorably on him years into the future.

Tactical Tip: Find something you're passionate about and put it to use online so you can put your best foot forward in a way that you're proud of.

Visit SafeSmartSocial.com/book to register this book for free and we will send you videos and key takeaways to help your students use social media to impress colleges and employers.

Key takeaways from this chapter:

- Whatever you do in real life will end up online. Get caught doing positive things.
- To make a lasting impression in whatever you do, you need to be confident in your ability, be passionate, and have a unique angle.
- Having a clean online image is going to add value to any organization that you are considering.
- "Anyone can feel comfortable and confident speaking to 1 or 1000 people, if they simply focus on what they do best and are passionate about in the world." – Dale Carnegie
- Find something you can do online that helps others and gives you a creative outlet to make a positive difference.
- Take your real life passion and realize that, with some hard work, it can end up helping you build a strong online image that might also inspire others, and will help you shine online.
- How you deal with real life struggles can be a great story to inspire others and motivate them with your positive approach.

BIBLIOGRAPHY

"Domino's Workers Disgusting YouTube Video: Spitting, Nose-Picking and Worse." Huffington Post. Last modified May 25, 2011.

Flacy, Mike. "Teenage Girl Posts Picture of Cash on Facebook, Family Robbed Within Hours." Digital   Trends. Last modified May 29, 2011.

Friedman, Emily. "Minn. High Schoolers Suspended for Facebook Pics." ABCNews.com.

"Gilbert Gottfried Fired As Aflac Duck After Tweet About Japanese Tsunami." Huffington Post Entertainment. last modified May 25, 2011.

"Kaplan Test Prep." Kaplan.com. Last modified October 31, 2013.

Luckerson, Victor. "When Colleges Look Up Applicants on Facebook: The Unspoken New Admissions Test." Time. Last modified November 15, 2012.

Ronson, Jon. "How One Stupid Tweet Blew Up Justine Sacco's Life." New York Times. Last modified February 12, 2015.

Saad, Nardine. "Glee Spoiler Extra Fired Nicole Crowther." Los Angeles Times. Last modified April 21, 2011.

Sanchez, Ray and Steffen, Sheila. "NY student accepted to all 8 Ivy League colleges picks Yale." CNN.com.

Singer, Natasha. "They Loved Your GPA Then They Saw Your Tweets." New York Times. Last modified November 9, 2013.

**All links can be found up-to-date at
SafeSmartSocial.com/research.**

SHARE YOUR PHOTO!

I want to meet my readers, especially you students! So, post your photos with this book and tag me on Twitter and Instagram with @JoshOchs.

I will share my favorites on social media and tag you, so that you can connect with like-minded parents and students who are also making changes to be Light, Bright, and Polite ®!

I will prepare and someday my chance will come.
–Abraham Lincoln

ISBN 978-0-9884039-6-3
$14.95
51495

LIGHT, BRIGHT & POLITE — JOSH OCHS

LIGHT
BRIGHT
&
POLITE

*How To Use Social Media
To Impress Colleges & Future Employers*

JOSH OCHS

ACKNOWLEDGMENTS

Thank you to the many people that were involved in the making of this book.

God – Thank you for blessing me with the great people and experiences who have helped me on my journey. It is because of you I have the strength to overcome obstacles and keep improving.

Mom and Dad – Thank you for giving me such a great work ethic, for always supporting me, for teaching me to take care of others and for always making sure I'm humble in all that I do.

My sisters Katie and Lacey – Thank you for always being a "voice of reason" and for keeping me grounded and helping me to stay honest.

Zack and Tex – Thank you for taking such great care of my sisters and for both becoming such great dads as you grow your families. I am very proud of both of you.

Jessica McIntyre – Thank you for all your support over the last 7+ years. You are an incredible friend and someone I can always count on.

Mollie McNally – Thank you for letting me share my message with your school and for coordinating a multi school speaking tour. Without your help I would have never retooled my content and found my niche.

Tracy Rampy – Thank you for believing in me and coordinating a Southeastern Kansas social media tour, letting me practice my message with thousands of students that

Greenbush serves. You are very fun to travel with and I'm confident that someday you'll learn how to hold my jacket without wrinkling it. ;)

Courtney Uebinger – Thank you for being so supportive during my speeches with Greenbush and for helping to coordinate press. Your efforts helped me to secure a news clip that has shared my message with thousands of families across the country.

Paula Little (and family) – Thank you for letting me stay at your home while I was practicing my content on thousands of students in the Blue Valley School District. Your family has been so gracious to me and you, perhaps, are the nicest person I've ever met. You are an inspiration to everyone, and I'm fortunate to have you as a cousin.

Marian Merritt – Thank you for supporting me from the very beginning by sending copies of your book to the hundreds of parents at my speeches. You have been instrumental in connecting me to influencers and guiding me through this online safety industry.

Kim Sanchez – Thank you for coordinating a Microsoft sponsorship for one of my speaking tours. With your help we were able to reach thousands of students across the Midwest how to shine online.

Jennifer Taylor – Thank you for letting me call you so many times and running many of my ideas by your kids to help me see if they are "cool" for the younger crowd. You have a wonderful attitude and I value your input.

James Todd – Thank you for connecting me with someone who contributed to this book. Also, thank you for helping me as I walked the streets of Barcelona. May you always find your five-iron golf club in the trunk of my car.

Anand Desai – Thank you for being such a great friend. You set a wonderful standard for all of us and I'm honored to be called "Uncle Josh" by your kids.

Matthew and Allyson Rener – Thank you for letting me practice my content with both of your daughters' Girl Scout groups and for connecting me with the local middle school to let me practice my message on my first 800 students. You helped me gain a lot of momentum.

Geoff Brown – You have been a great friend over the years offering me ideas and suggestions as we refine our content and brainstorm new ideas. You're one of the smartest guys I know and I appreciate your friendship.

Minling Chuang – Thank you for encouraging me to plan out my goals and for helping me to dream big.

Camille Marquez – Thank you for being such a hard worker and giving me feedback as we launch this teen/tween program. I'm so proud of all the work you're doing and excited to see how quickly your hard work pays off in your career.

Anastasiia Demydenko – You have helped to organize me and create dozens of helpful online safety videos. Without your help I would not be able to create the content that has helped over 20,000 people on the web.

Deanna Mehlhoff – Thank you for helping me to form my thoughts and words in this book. With your help I have been able to articulate each of my ideas into something that can help others.

Ben Knapik – Thank you for being so supportive of all the fun projects I work on. Your positive attitude is a great source of inspiration.

Suzy Zaifert – Thank you for working with me to design this content for kids and letting me launch it at Universal Studios with hundreds of kids. Without your idea, I may not have retooled my content to start working on students. I appreciate your support.

Misty Burke – Thank you for letting me share my message at your conference and connecting me with your daughter's school to make a positive impact on their student body. I appreciate your support.

Stephen Balkam – Thank you for connecting me with some of the contributors of this book. Your work at FOSI is terrific and you are helping countless families around the world to be safer online.

ABOUT JOSH OCHS

Josh Ochs combines his background in marketing at Disney and his love for all things technology to help teens and tweens use social media as a portfolio of positive accomplishments. Josh travels the nation speaking to over 15,000 kids each year, sharing tips they can use to create a positive online presence. Josh's 2015 book, *Light, Bright and Polite*, shows students exactly what they should post on social media to impress colleges and employers, explaining practical examples to create a resume that lets them own the first page of their online search results.

In 2009, Josh was nearly elected to Hermosa Beach, CA city council, gaining 70% of the votes required to win a seat in the local election against the incumbent mayor. As the youngest person on the ballot with limited resources, Josh assembled a grassroots team to help him canvas over 3,000 homes to meet voters on their doorsteps, followed with social media outreach. Now, Josh and his team advise politicians, professionals and families nationwide on how they can use digital tools to impress customers, colleges and employers.

Quoted and featured as a source in Forbes, CBS News, KTLA, KFWB radio, Josh is a guest lecturer at USC and UCLA and a frequent personality on radio shows nationwide. He lives and works in Los Angeles where he was born and raised.

Get In Touch:

- Request Josh to speak at your school by emailing Book@SafeSmartSocial.com
- Watch free online safety videos from Josh's team: SafeSmartSocial.com
- Connect with Josh at LinkedIn.com/in/joshochs
- Learn more about Josh at JoshOchs.com

NOTES

NOTES

** Include #LightBrightPolite
or tag @JoshOchs with your
Twitter, Facebook or Instagram pics.*

NOTES

* Include #LightBrightPolite
or tag @JoshOchs with your
Twitter, Facebook or Instagram pics.

— 160 —

NOTES

NOTES

INCLUDE #LightBrightPolite
OR TAG @JoshOchs WITH YOUR
TWITTER, FACEBOOK OR INSTAGRAM PICS.

CPSIA information can be obtained at www.ICGtesting.com
Printed in the USA
LVOW04s1539190815

450752LV00022B/1825/P